Voice Training:

A Primer for Better Speaking and Singing

Marlo Hendrix, PH.D

With text and notes

THOMAS FILLEBROWN, M.D., D.M.D.

NMD Books

Simi Valley, CA

Visit our Web site at http://www.NMDbooks.com.

Library of Congress Cataloging-in-Publication Data

Voice Training A Primer For Better Speaking and Singing

ISBN: 978-1-936828-18-0 (Softcover)

CONTENTS

INTRODUCTION

WHEN a youth it was my lot to be surrounded by examples of faulty vocalism, such as prevailed in a country town, and to be subjected to the errors then in vogue, having at the same time small opportunity for training in the application of principles, even as then imperfectly taught. At middle life I had given up all attempt at singing and had difficulty in speaking so as to be heard at any considerable distance or for any considerable length of time. Professional obligations to my patients, however, compelled me later to take up the subject of vocal physiology. This I did, guided by the ideas current on the subject.

About 1880 I became satisfied that many of the current ideas were incorrect, and determined to start anew, and to note in detail the action of each organ used in vocalization and articulation. To this end I sought vocal instruction and advice, which, modified by my own observations, have produced the most gratifying results.

Up to that time it had been held that the nasal cavities must be cut off from the mouth by the closing of the soft palate against the back of the throat; that the passage of ever so little of the sound above the palate would give a nasal twang, and that the sound was reinforced and developed only in the cavities of the throat and mouth. My practice in Oral[Pg 2] Surgery, coupled with my own vocal studies exposed this fallacy and revealed to me the true value of nasal resonance.

The late Mme. Rudersdorff had begun to recognize the effect of nasal resonance, but she left no published record of her conclusions. It does not appear that she or her contemporaries realized the true value of the nasal and head cavities as reinforcing agents in the production of tone, or appreciated their influence upon its quality and power.

There are perhaps few subjects on which a greater variety of opinion exists than on that of voice culture, and few upon which so many volumes have been written. Few points are uncontested, and exactly opposite statements are made in regard to each.

Formerly great stress was laid upon the distinction between "head tones" and "chest tones," "closed tones" and "open tones." The whole musical world was in bondage to "registers of the voice," and the one great task confronting the singer and vocal teacher was to "blend the registers," a feat still baffling the efforts of many instructors.

Many teachers and singers have now reached what they consider a demonstrated conclusion that registers are not a natural feature of the voice; yet a large contingent still adhere to the doctrine of "register," depending for their justification upon the unreliable evidence furnished by the laryngoscope, not realizing that there will be found in the little lens as many different conditions as the observers have eyes to see. Garcia himself, the inventor of the laryngoscope, soon modified his first claims as to its value in vocal culture.

On this point we have the testimony of his biographer, M.S. McKinley:

"As far as Garcia was concerned, the laryngoscope ceased to be of any special use as soon as his first investigations were concluded. By his examination of the glottis he had the satisfaction of proving that all his theories with regard to the emission of the voice were absolutely correct. Beyond that[Pg 3] he did not see that anything further was to be gained except to satisfy the curiosity of those who might be interested in seeing for themselves the forms and changes which the inside of the larynx assumed during singing and speaking."

Of similar purport is the word of the eminent baritone, Sir Charles Santley, who, in his *Art of Singing*, says:

"Manuel Garcia is held up as the pioneer of scientific teaching of singing. He was—but he taught singing, not surgery! I was a pupil of his in 1858 and a friend of his while he lived;[1] and in all the conversations I had with him I never heard him say a word about larynx or pharynx, glottis or any other organ used in the production and emission of the voice. He was perfectly acquainted with their functions, but he used his knowledge for his own direction, not to parade it before his pupils."

The eminent London surgeon and voice specialist, Dr. Morell Mackenzie, says of the laryngoscope, "It can scarcely be said to have thrown any new light on the mechanism of the voice"; and Dr. Lennox Browne confesses that, "Valuable as has been the laryngoscope in a physiological, as undoubtedly it is in a medical sense, it has been the means of making all theories of voice production too dependent on the vocal cords, and thus the importance of the other parts of the vocal apparatus has been overlooked."

Not only in regard to "registers" but in regard to resonance, focus, articulation, and the offices and uses of the various vocal organs, similar antagonistic opinions exist. Out of this chaos must some time come a demonstrable system.

A generation ago the art of breathing was beginning to be more an object of study, but the true value of correct lateral abdominal breathing was by no means generally admitted or appreciated. It was still taught that the larynx (voice-box) should bob up and down like a jack-in-a-box with each change of pitch, and that "female breathing" must be performed[Pg 4] with a pumping action of the chest and the elevation and depression of the collar bone.

Fortunately, teachers and singers recognized a good tone when they heard it, and many taught much better than they knew, so that the public did not have to wait for the development of accurate knowledge of the subject before hearing excellent singing and speaking. Yet many singers had their voices ruined in the training, and their success as vocalists made impossible; while others, a little less unfortunate, were still handicapped through life by the injury done by mistaken methods in early years. Jenny Lind's perfect vocal organs were quite disabled at twelve years of age by wrong methods, and they recovered only after a protracted season of rest. As a consequence her beautiful voice began to fail long before her splendid physique, and long before her years demanded. Singers taught in nature's way should be able to sing so long as strength lasts, and, like Adelaide Phillips, Carl Formes, and Sims Reeves, sing their sweetest songs in the declining years of life. Martel, at seventy years of age, had a full, rich voice. He focused all his tones alike, and employed deep abdominal breathing.

The whole matter of voice training has been clouded by controversy. The strident advocates of various systems, each of them "the only true method," have in their disputes overcast the subject with much that is irrelevant, thus obscuring its essential simplicity.

The "scientific" teachers, at one extreme, have paid too exclusive attention to the mechanics of the voice. The "empiricists" have gone to the other extreme in leaving out of account fundamental facts in acoustics, physiology, and psychology.

The truth is that no purely human function, especially one so subtle as singing, can be developed mechanically; nor, on the other hand, can the mere *ipse dixit* of any teacher satisfy the demands of the modern spirit.

PRINCIPLES ADVOCATED

The positions here advocated, because they seem both rational and simple, are:

1. That the singing and speaking tones are identical, produced by the same organs in the same way, and developed by the same training.

2. That breathing is, for the singer, only an amplification of the correct daily habit.

3. That "registers" are a myth.

4. That "head tones, chest tones, closed tones, open tones," etc., as confined to special parts of the range of the voice, are distracting distinctions arising from false education.

5. That resonance determines the quality and carrying power of every tone, and is therefore the most important element in the study and training of the voice.

6. That the obstacles to good speaking and singing are psychologic rather than physiologic.

7. That, in the nature of things, the right way is always an easy way.

CHAPTER I
THE VOCAL INSTRUMENT

SINCE the vocal organism first became an object of systematic study, discussion has been constant as to whether the human vocal instrument is a stringed instrument, a reed instrument, or a whistle. Discussion of the question seems futile, for practically it is all of these and more. The human vocal organs form an instrument, *sui generis,* which cannot be compared with any other one thing. Not only is it far more complex than any other instrument, being capable, as it is, of imitating nearly every instrument in the catalogue and almost every sound in nature, but it is incomparably more beautiful, an instrument so universally superior to any made by man that comparisons and definitions fail.

ELEMENTS

The human vocal instrument has the three elements common to all musical instruments,—a motor, a vibrator, and a resonator; to which is added—what all other instruments lack—an articulator.

1. The respiratory muscles and lungs for a **motor**.

2. The vocal cords for a **vibrator**.

3. The throat, mouth, and the nasal and head cavities for a **resonator**.

4. The tongue, lips, teeth, and palate for an **articulator**.

These elements appear in as great a variety of size and proportion as do the variations of individual humanity, and each element is, moreover, variable according to the will or feeling of the individual. This susceptibility to change constitutes a modifying power which gives a variety in tone quality possible to no other instrument and makes it our wonder and[Pg 7] admiration. The modification and interaction of these various parts produced by the emotions of the singer or speaker give qualities of tone expressive of the feelings, as of pain or pleasure, grief or joy, courage or fear.

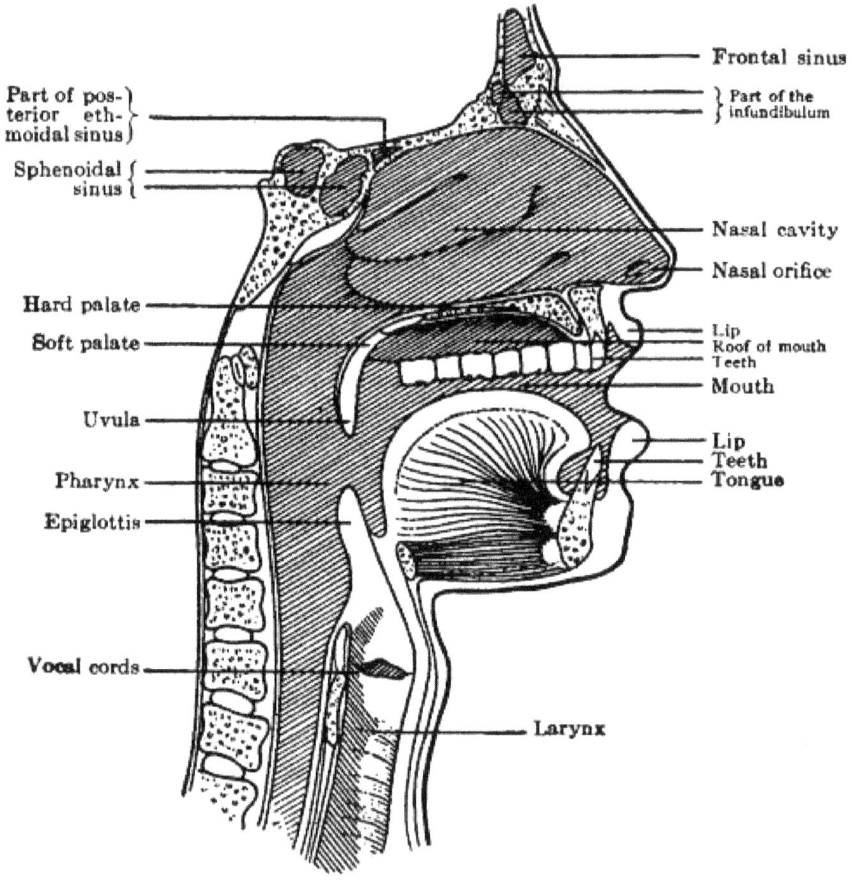

FIGURE 1.—Section of the head and throat locating the organs of speech and song, including the upper resonators. The important maxillary sinus cannot well be shown. It is found within the maxillary bone (cheek bone). The inner end of the line marked *Nasal cavity* locates it.

TIMBRE

The minute differences in these physical conditions, coupled with the subtler differences in the psychical elements of the personality, account for that distinctive physiognomy of the voice called **timbre**, which is only another name for individuality as exhibited in each person. The same general elements enter into the composition of all voices, from the basso profundo to the high soprano.

That the reader may better understand the proportion and relations of the different parts of the vocal apparatus, a sectional drawing of the head is here produced, showing the natural position of the vocal organs at rest. As the drawing represents but a vertical section of the head the reader should note that the sinuses, like the eyes and nostrils, lie in pairs to the right and left of the centre of the face. The location of the maxillary sinuses within the maxillary or cheek bones cannot be shown in this drawing.

The dark shading represents the cavities of the throat, nose, and head. The relations of the parts are shown more accurately than is possible in any diagram. It will be noticed that the vibrations from the larynx would pass directly behind the soft palate into the nasal chamber, and very directly into the mouth. The nasal roof is formed by two bones situated between the eyes; the sphenoid or wedge-bone, which is connected with all other bones of the head, and the ethmoid or sieve-like bone. The structure of these two bones, especially of the ethmoid, consists of very thin plates or laminæ, forming a mass of air cavities which communicate by small openings with the nasal cavity below. Thus, the vibrations in the nose are transmitted to the air spaces above, and the effective qualities of the head vibrations are added to the tone.

THE LARYNX

The larynx or voice-box contains the vocal cords. Just above the vocal cords on each side is a large, deep cavity, called the ventricle. These cavities reinforce the primary vibrations set up by the cords and serve to increase their intensity as they are projected from the larynx. The larynx is the vibrating organ of the voice. It is situated at the base of the tongue and is so closely connected with it by attachment to the hyoid bone, to which the tongue is also attached, that it is capable of only slight movement independent of that organ; consequently it must move with the tongue in articulation. The interior muscles of the larynx vary the position of its walls, thus regulating the proximity and tension of the vocal cords. The male larynx is the larger and shows the Adam's apple. In both sexes the larynx of the low voice, alto or bass, is larger than that of the high voice, soprano or tenor. The larynx and tongue should not rise with the pitch of the voice, but drop naturally with the lower jaw as the mouth opens in ascending the scale. The proper position of the tongue will insure a proper position for the larynx. The less attention the larynx receives the better.

THE VOCAL CORDS

The vocal cords are neither cords nor bands, but instead are thick portions of membrane extending across the inner surface of the larynx. On account of familiarity the name *vocal cords* will still be used. They are fairly well represented by the lips of the cornet player when placed on the mouthpiece of the instrument. The pitch of the tone is fixed by the tension of the vocal cords and the width and length of the opening between them. Their tension and proximity are self-adjusted to produce the proper pitch without any conscious volition of the singer. They can have no special training, needing only to be left alone. The work of the vocal cords, though essentially important, is, when naturally performed, light and consequently not exhausting. If the larynx and all of its supporting muscles are relaxed as they are in free and easy breathing, then when the air passes out through the larynx, the vocal cords will automatically assume a tension sufficient to vocalize the breath and give the note the proper pitch. The normal action of the cords will never cause hoarseness or discomfort. The sound should seem to be formed, not in the throat,—thus involving the vocal cords,—but in the resonance chambers.

THE EPIGLOTTIS

The epiglottis is the valve which closes over the upper opening of the larynx. It not only closes the mouth of the larynx when food is swallowed, but aids materially in converting into tone the vibrations set up by the vocal cords.

THE PHARYNX

The pharynx extends from the larynx to the nasal cavity. The size of the opening into the nasal chamber is controlled by the soft palate and is frequently entirely closed. The size of the pharynx is varied by the contraction and relaxation of the circular muscles in its tissue; when swallowing its walls are in contact. The pharynx acts as does the expanding tube of brass instruments. It increases the force and depth of the tone waves. The wider the pharynx is opened, without constraint, the fuller the resonance and the better the tone.

THE UNDER JAW

The under jaw furnishes attachment for the muscles of the tongue and hyoid or tongue bone. It also controls, owing to the connections of the larynx with the hyoid bone, the muscles that fix the position of the larynx.

The pterygoid muscles, which move the under jaw forward and backward, do not connect with the larynx, so their action does not compress that organ or in any way impede the action of the vocal apparatus. A relaxed under jaw allows freer action of the vocal cords and ampler resonance. The under jaw should drop little by little as the voice ascends the scale, thus opening the mouth slightly wider with each rise in the pitch of the tone. In ascending the scale it is well to open the throat a little wider as you ascend. The delivery will be much easier, and the tone produced will be much better. At the highest pitch of the voice the mouth should open to its full width. At the same time care must be taken *not* to draw the corners of the mouth back, as in smiling, because this lessens the resonance of the tone and gives it a flat sound.

The under jaw must have considerable latitude of motion in pronunciation, but by all means avoid chewing of the words and cutting off words by closing the jaw instead of finishing them by the use of the proper articulating organs, which are the tongue and lips.

THE SOFT PALATE

Writers on the voice have almost universally claimed that the principal office of the soft palate is to shut off the nasal and head cavities from the throat, and to force the column of vibrations out through the mouth, thus allowing none, or at most a very small part, to pass into the nasal passages.

This contention implies that the vibrations are imparted to the upper cavities, if at all, through the walls of the palate itself, and not through an opening behind the palate. This is entirely at variance with the facts as verified by my own experience and observation and the observation of others who are expert specialists. The true office of the soft palate is to modify the opening into the nose and thus attune the resonant cavities to the pitch and timbre of the note given by the vocal cords and pharynx. To develop the vowel sounds, the soft palate should be drawn forward, allowing a free passage into the nose; it should be closed only to form the consonants which require a forcible expulsion of breath from the mouth.

The uvula, the pendulous tip of the soft palate, serves as a valve to more accurately adjust the opening behind the soft palate to the pitch of the voice. In producing a low tone the soft palate is relaxed and hangs low down and far forward. As the voice ascends the scale the tension of the soft palate is increased and it is elevated and the uvula shortened, thus decreasing the opening behind the palate, but never closing it. In fact the larger the opening that can be maintained, the broader and better the tone. The author was himself unable fully to appreciate this until he had become able to sense the position of the soft palate during vocalization.

THE HARD PALATE AND TEETH

The hard palate and upper teeth form in part the walls of the mouth. As they are solid fixtures, nothing can be done in the way of training. They furnish a point of impingement in articulation, and play their part in sympathetic resonance.

The bones which form the roof of the mouth serve also for the floor of the nasal cavity.

The under teeth also serve as walls of resistance to support the tongue during the performance of its functions.

THE NASAL AND HEAD CAVITIES

The nasal and head cavities are resonating chambers incapable of special training, but their form, size, and the use made of them have a wonderful effect upon the resonance of the voice. If the vibrations are strong here, all other parts will vibrate in harmonious action.

When responding to the perfectly focused tone the thin walls of the cavities and the contained air vibrate with surprising force, often for the moment blinding the singer when sounding a note intensely.

Having in my surgical work demonstrated the existence of a hitherto unrecognized connecting passage or canal between the air cavities of the face and those of the forehead,[2] the play of resonance in the cavities above the nostrils is more easily understood. The function of the cavities known as the *frontal sinuses* (see Fig. 1) has long been a mystery, but now that their direct connection with the lower cavities is proven, and the great significance of resonance is also beginning to be recognized, the mystery disappears. The same may be said of the other sinuses—*ethmoidal, sphenoidal,* and *maxillary,* and their interconnection.

INFLUENCE OF THE RESONANCE CAVITIES ON THE PITCH OF THE TONE

In instruments changes in the length and form of the resonance chambers affect the pitch as well as the quality of the tone. This is demonstrated in the trombone, French horn, and other wind instruments. The lengthening of the tube of the trombone lowers the pitch of the tone, and the projection of the hand of the performer into the bell of the French horn has the effect of raising the pitch of the sound. If the variation in length or form is only slight, the result is sharp or flat, and the instrument is out of tune. In the human instrument all the organs act together as a unit; so the fact that the cavities alone may affect the pitch is practically of no great significance.

THE TONGUE

The tongue and the lips are the articulating organs, and the former has an important part to play in altering through its movements the shape of the mouth cavity.

The tip of the tongue should habitually rest against the under front teeth. The tip of the tongue, however, must frequently touch the roof of the mouth near the upper front teeth, as when pronouncing the consonants *c, d, g* or *j, l, n, s,* and *t*. The back part of the tongue must rise a little to close against the soft palate when pronouncing *g* hard, and *k*, and hard *c*, *q*, and *x*. The soft palate comes down so far to meet the tongue that the elevation of the latter need be but very slight.

When speaking, the demand is not so imperative, but when singing, the body of the tongue should lie as flat as possible, so as to enlarge the mouth, especially when giving the vowel sounds.

If the tongue is sometimes disposed to be unruly, it is the result of rigidity or misplaced effort in the surrounding parts. This tendency will only be aggravated by artificial restraint of any kind. The true way is to dismiss tongue consciousness, *let go*, and a normal flexibility will easily manifest itself.[Pg 14]

THE LIPS

The lips, equally with the tongue, are organs of articulation. The upper lip is the principal factor of the two; the under lip seems to follow the lead of the upper. The lips need much training, and it can readily be given them. While practising to educate the lips, both lips should be projected forward and upward, at the same time pronouncing the word "too." Bring the edge of the upper lip as high toward the nose as possible in practice.

This will bring the corners of the mouth forward and lift the lips clear and free from the teeth, and thus add one more resonance cavity. This position of the lips also gives freedom for pronunciation. "The upper lip plays the most active part in the shaping of the vowels.

It should never be drawn against the teeth when producing vowel tones; indeed, there should be often a little space between the upper lip and the teeth, so that the vibrations of the sound-waves can have free play."

THE NOSTRILS

The nostrils should be dilated as much as possible, as a free, wide, open nose gives a free, well-rounded tone, while a contracted nostril induces the nasal tone so much dreaded. A proper training of the facial muscles makes this dilation possible. Lifting the upper lip and projecting it forward aids the action to a great degree.

There is a strong tendency to unity of action between the nostrils and the lips and the soft palate. The soft palate moves downward and forward when the upper lip protrudes and the nostrils dilate, and moves backward and upward when the nostrils are contracted and the upper lip allowed to rest upon the teeth.

As a rule the best singers have full, round, wide, open nostrils, either given by nature or acquired by practice.

THE FACE

Not only must the lips and nose be trained, but the muscles of the face also. These muscles are capable, if educated, of doing important service.

The artist on the operatic stage or the speaker on the platform, without facial expression begotten of muscular activity, may lessen by half his power over an audience. To train the facial muscles is a complicated task. To do this, stand before a mirror and make all the faces ever thought of by a schoolboy to amuse his schoolmates. Raise each corner of the lip, wrinkle the nose, quilt the forehead, grin, laugh. The grimaces will not enter into a performance, but their effect upon it will be markedly beneficial.

CHAPTER II

THE SPEAKING VOICE AND PRONUNCIATION

A GENERATION ago the speaking voice was even less understood than the singing voice. That the two were intimately connected was but half surmised. Only an occasional person recognized what is now generally conceded, that a good way to improve the speaking voice is to cultivate the singing voice.

I published a paper in the *Independent Practitioner* defining the singing voice and the speaking voice as identical, and contending that the training for each should be the same so far as tone formation is involved, a conclusion at which I had arrived several years before. Subsequent experience has only served to confirm this opinion.

The past has produced many good speakers, among them Henry Clay, Daniel Webster, Edwin Booth, Wm. Charles Macready, and Edward Everett. Of the last Oliver Wendell Holmes wrote: "It is with delight that one who remembers Edward Everett in his robes of rhetorical splendor, recalls his full blown, high colored, double flowered periods; the rich, resonant, grave, far-reaching music of his speech, with just enough of the nasal vibration to give the vocal sounding-board its proper value in the harmonies of utterance." These examples of correct vocalization, however, were exceptions to the general rule; they happened to speak well, but the physiologic action of the vocal organs which produced such results in those individual cases was not understood, and hence the pupil ambitious to imitate them and develop the best of which his voice was capable had no rule by which to proceed. Few could speak with ease, still fewer could be heard by a large assembly, and sore throats seemed to be the rule.

DIFFERENCE BETWEEN SINGING AND SPEAKING

In singing the flow of tone is unbroken between the words, but in speaking it is interrupted. In singing tone is sustained and changed from one pitch to another by definite intervals over a wide compass that includes notes not attempted in speech. In speaking tone is unsustained, not defined in pitch, is limited to a narrow compass, and the length of the tones is not governed by the measure of music.

Notwithstanding these differences, singing and speaking tones are produced by the vocal organs in the same way, are focused precisely alike, have the same resonance, and are delivered in the same manner. It has been said that speech differs from song as walking from dancing. Speech may be called the prose, and song the poetry of vocalization.

During the past decade the knowledge of the speaking voice has been greatly broadened, and the art of cultivating tone has made progress. The identity of the singing and speaking voice is becoming more fully recognized, and methods are being used to develop the latter similar to those in use for the training of the former. As Dr. Morell Mackenzie says: "Singing is a help to good speaking, as the greater includes the less."

The recognition of this truth cannot fail to be a great aid to the progress of singing in the public schools, since every enlargement of exercises common to both speaking and singing helps to solidarity and *esprit de corps* in teaching and in learning.

An accurate sense of pitch, melody, harmony, and rhythm is necessary to the singer, but the orator may, by cultivation, develop a speaking voice of musical quality without being able to distinguish *Old Hundred* from *The Last Rose of Summer*.

PRONUNCIATION

It is a matter of common observation that American singers, although they may be painstaking in their French and German, are indifferent, even to carelessness, in the clear and[Pg 18] finished enunciation of their native tongue. Mr. W.J. Henderson, in his recent work, *The Art of the Singer*, says: "The typical American singer cannot sing his own language so that an audience can understand him; nine-tenths of the songs we hear are songs without words." Happily this condition is gradually yielding to a better one, stimulated in part by the examples of visiting singers and actors. In story-telling songs and in oratorio, slovenly delivery is reprehensible, but when the words of a song are the lyric flight of a true poet, a careless utterance becomes intolerable.

Beauty of tone is not everything; the singing of mere sounds, however lovely, is but a tickling of the ear. The shortcoming of the Italian school of singing, as of composition, has been too exclusive devotion to sensuous beauty of tone as an end in itself. The singer must never forget that his mission is to **vitalize text with tone**. The songs of Schubert, Schumann, Franz, Brahms, Grieg, Strauss, and Wolf, as well as the Wagnerian drama, are significant in their inseparable union of text and music. The singer is therefore an interpreter, not of music alone, but of text made potent by music.

Pronunciation, moreover, concerns not only the listener, but the singer and speaker, for pure tone and pure pronunciation cannot be divorced, one cannot exist without the other. In his interesting work, *The Singing of the Future*, Mr. Ffrangcon-Davies insists that, "the quickest way to fine tone is through fine pronunciation."

We cannot think except in words, nor voice our thought without speech. Vocal utterance is thought articulate. Therefore, instead of prolonged attention to tone itself, training should be concentrated upon the uttered word. The student should aim "to sing a word rather than a tone." Correct pronunciation and beautiful tone are so interdependent as to be inseparable.

The singer and speaker require all sounds in their purity. To seek to develop the voice along the narrow limits of any single vowel or syllable, as for instance the syllable *ah*, is harm[Pg 19]ful. Not only is this vowel sound, as Lilli Lehmann says, "the most difficult," but the proper pronunciation of all words within the whole range of the voice is thereby impeded. Diction and tone work should therefore go hand in hand. "The way in which vowel melts into vowel and consonants float into their places largely determines the character of the tone itself." Without finished pronunciation speech and song of emotional power are impossible. Gounod, the composer, says, "Pronunciation creates eloquence." Mr. Forbes-Robertson, the English master of dramatic diction, speaking for his own profession says: "The trouble with contemporary stage elocution springs from the actor's very desire to act well. In his effort to be natural he mumbles his words as too many people do in everyday life. Much of this can be corrected by constantly bearing in mind the true value of vowels, the percussive value of consonants, and the importance of keeping up the voice until the last word is spoken. There must be, so to speak, plenty of wind in the bellows. The great thing is to have the sound come from the front of the mouth.... The actor must learn to breathe deeply from the diaphragm and to take his breath at the proper time. Too often the last word is not held up, and that is very often the important word.... Schools for acting are valuable, ... but, after all, the actors, like other folk, must be taught how to speak as children in the home, at school, and in society."

In pronunciation the words should seem to be formed by the upper lip and to come out through it. By this method it will be found easy to pronounce distinctly. The words will thus be formed outside the mouth and be readily heard, as is a person talking in front of, instead of behind, a screen. A single, intelligent trial will be sufficient to show the correctness of the statement. Thinking of the upper lip as the fashioner of the words makes speaking easy and singing a delight.

To smile while talking gives to the words a flat, silly sound, hence the corners of the mouth should be kept well forward.[Pg 20]

THE SINGER'S SCALE OF VOWEL SOUNDS

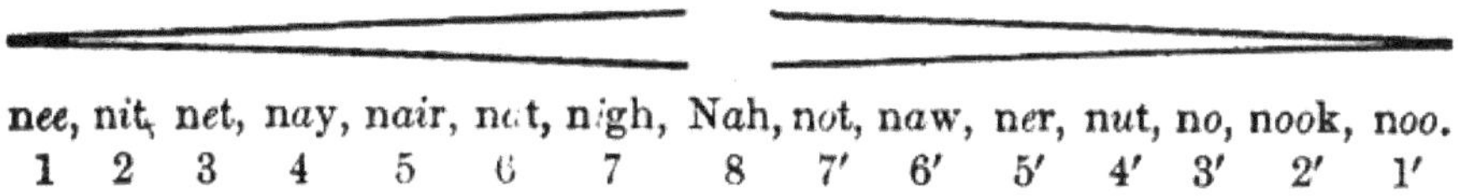

It may fasten this in mind to remember that at one end of the vowel scale is—*me*, at the other—*you*.

The teeth and lips are most closed at the extremes of this scale, and gradually open toward *ah*, with which vowel they are widest apart.

In the series 1-8 the tongue is highest in the centre for *ee* and gradually descends until it lies flat in the mouth for *ah*.

The *upper* pharynx is most closed in 1, most open in 8, and closes more and more in the descending series 7'-1'.

The *lower* pharynx gradually opens in the descending series 7'-1'.

The researches of Helmholtz, Koenig, Willis, Wheatstone, Appunn, Bell, and others have shown that each vowel sound has its own characteristic pitch. The Scale of Vowel Sounds given above corresponds closely to the order of resonance pitch from the highest *ee* to the lowest *oo*. In the natural resonance of the vowels *ee* is highest in the head, *ah* is midway in the scale, and *oo* is lowest in resonance.

LIP POSITION

Figure 2 shows the best position of the lips to give the sound of *ee*. Hold the under jaw without stiffness and as far from the upper teeth as is consistent with delivery of the pure sound of this vowel.

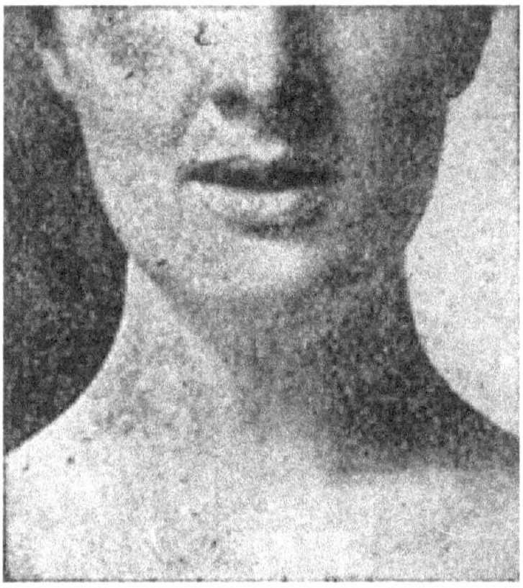

FIGURE 2.

Figure 3 shows the best position of the lips to produce the vowel *oo*.

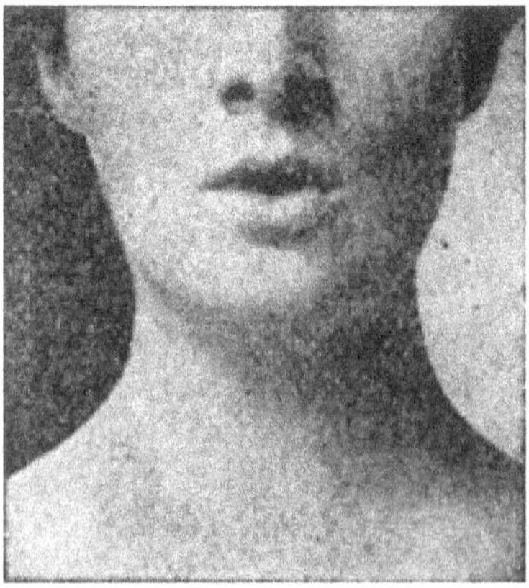

FIGURE 3.

Figure 4 shows the position of the lips for the vowel sound of long *o*. The opening of the lips should be made as round as is the letter *o*. When preparing the lips to give the sound of *o*, the inclination is strong to drop the lower jaw; in practice, to develop action of the lips, the under jaw would better be[Pg 21] held quite immovable. It will be found possible to produce all of the vowel sounds without any change except in the form of the opening of the lips. The vowel sound of *i* is an exception; for as a compound of *ah* and *ee*, the extremes of the vowel scale, it requires two distinct positions for its utterance with a movement of transition between; it is not, therefore, a good vowel for initial practice.

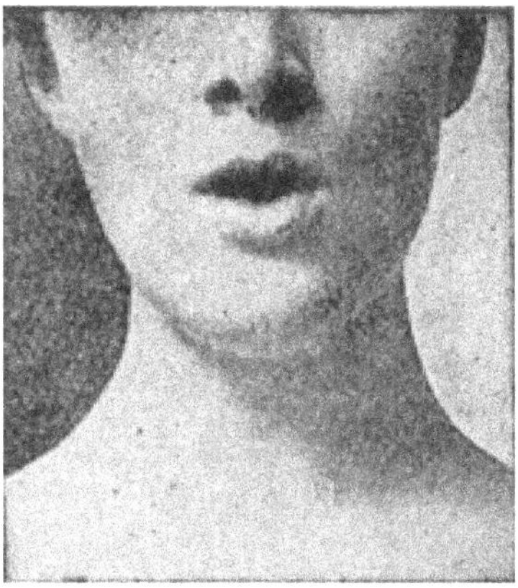

FIGURE 4.

Figure 5 shows that the sound *aw* is produced from *o* by raising the edge of the upper lip outward and upward, and flattening the raised portion laterally.[Pg 22]

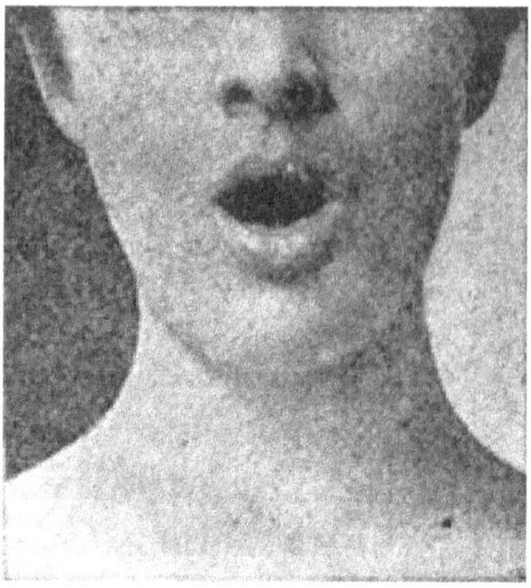

FIGURE 5.

Figure 6 shows the position for producing *ah*. It differs from the position assumed for *aw* in that the opening of the lips is larger, the upper lip is raised higher, the flat portion is wider, and the under lip is a little relaxed. The form of the opening to produce *aw* is oval; the form for *ah* is more nearly square.

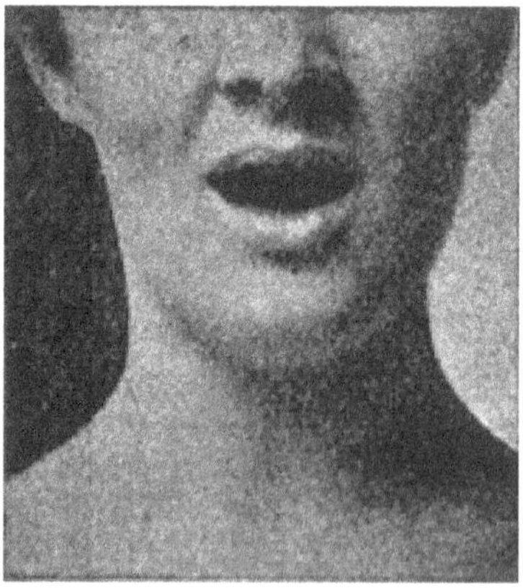

FIGURE 6.

Figure 7 shows the under jaw relaxed, as it should be in practice, to enlarge the throat and give roundness and largeness to the tone. The use of the word *hung* will accomplish this end.

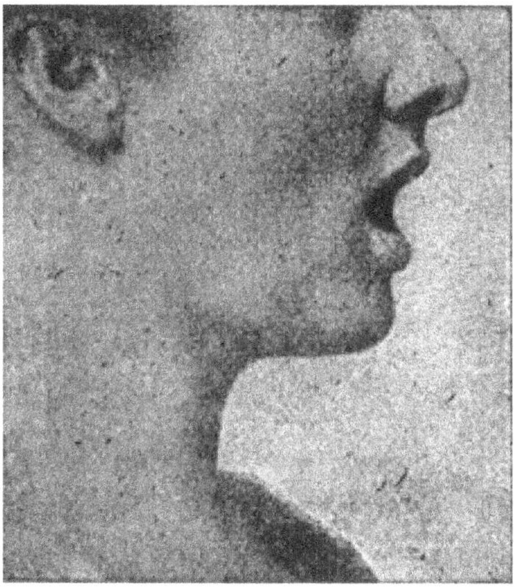

FIGURE 7.

The vowel sounds illustrated above are embodied in a series of vocal exercises to be found in Chapter VIII on *Placing the Voice*.

CHAPTER III
BREATH CONTROL

IT has been said that "breathing is singing." This statement is equally applicable to speaking. While the aphorism is not literally true, it is true that without properly controlled breathing the best singing or speaking tone cannot be produced, for tone is but vocalized breath; hence in the cultivation of the voice, breathing is the first function to receive attention.

For singer or speaker, the correct use of the breathing apparatus determines the question of success or failure; for without mastery of the motive power all else is unavailing. For a voice user, therefore, the first requisite is a well-developed chest, the second, complete control of it.

It must not be supposed that a singer's breathing is something strange or complex, for it is nothing more than *an amplification of normal, healthy breathing*. In contrast, however, to the undisciplined casual breathing of the general public, the singer is a professional breather.

THE MUSCLES OF RESPIRATION

There are two sets of respiratory muscles, one for inspiration and another for expiration,—twenty-two or more in all. The principal muscles of inspiration are the diaphragm and the intercostal muscles that elevate the ribs. The chief muscles of expiration are the four sets of abdominal muscles and the intercostal muscles that depress the ribs. The diaphragm is *not* a muscle of *expiration*.

THE DIAPHRAGM

The diaphragm is in form like an inverted bowl (Fig. 8). It forms the floor of the thorax (chest) and the roof of the[Pg 24] abdomen. It is attached by a strong tendon to the spinal column behind, and to the walls of the thorax at its lowest part, which is below the ribs. In front its attachment is to the cartilage at the pit of the stomach. It also connects with the transverse abdominal muscle. The diaphragm being convex, in inspiration the contraction of its fibres flattens it downward and presses down the organs in the abdomen, thus increasing the depth of the thorax. Expiration depends wholly on other muscles.

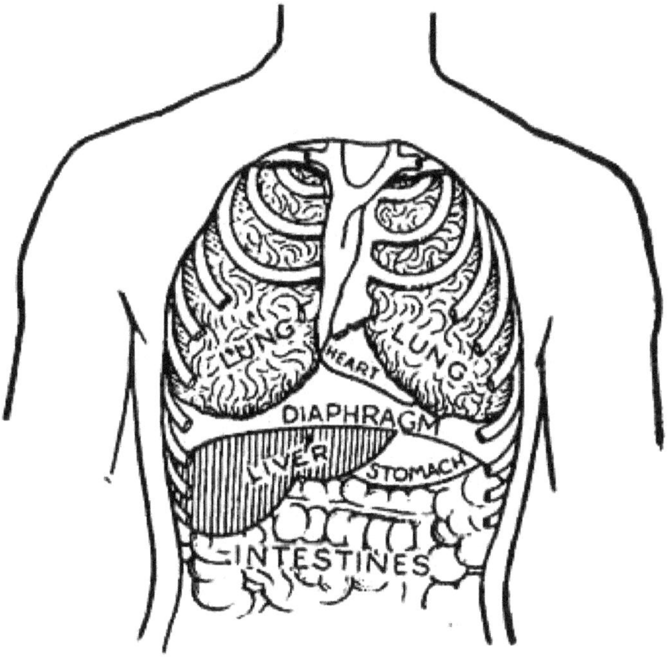

FIGURE 8.

The muscles so far mentioned are all that need "conscious education;" the others will act with them voluntarily, automatically. The abdominal muscles relax during inspiration and the diaphragm relaxes during expiration, thus rendering the forces nearly equal, though the strength is in favor of the expiratory muscles. This is what is needed, for the breath while speaking or singing must go out under much greater tension than is necessary for inhalation. Inspiration should be as free as possible from obstruction when singing or speaking. Expiration must be under *controlled* pressure.

THE LUNGS

The lungs are spongy bodies which have no activity of their own beyond a little elasticity. They are controlled by the muscles of respiration.

Figure 8 shows the organs of the body in their natural positions. The diaphragm is relaxed and curved upward, as in expiration. During inspiration the diaphragm is drawn down until it lies nearly flat.

INSPIRATION

The intercostal muscles raise the ribs. The diaphragm is drawn down by contraction, thus adding to the enlargement of the chest by increasing its depth. The abdominal muscles relax and allow the stomach, liver, and other organs in the abdomen to move downward to make room for the depressed diaphragm. This causes a vacuum in the chest. The lungs expand to fill this vacuum and the air rushes in to fill the expanding lungs.

EXPIRATION

The intercostal, and a part of the abdominal, muscles depress the ribs and lessen the chest cavity anteriorly and laterally. The abdominal muscles compress the abdomen and force up the diaphragm which is now relaxed, thus lessening the depth of the thorax. This pressure forces the air from the lungs and prepares them for another inspiration.

CORRECT METHOD

That the lateral-abdominal—more accurately chest-abdominal—breathing is correct and natural for both male, and female, and that the shoulders should remain as fixed as were Demosthenes' under the points of the swords hung over them, is now so generally admitted as to need no argument here. If any one has still a doubt on the subject let him observe a sleeping infant. It affords a perfect example of lateral-abdominal breathing, and no one can have a suspicion of sex from[Pg 26] any difference in this function. Among the lower animals sex shows no difference in breathing at any age. All the peculiarities of female breathing are the results of habits acquired in after life.

Chest and shoulder heaving are vicious and evidence impeded breathing. The singer who, forgetting the lower thorax, breathes with the upper only is sure to fail. Therefore breathe from the *lower* part of the trunk, using the whole muscular system coördinately—*from below* upward. In other words breathe deeply, and *control deeply*, but with the whole body—from below, not with the upper chest only, or with lateral expansion only, or abdominal expansion only.

Every teacher and pupil should remember that "singing and speaking require wind and muscle," hence the breathing power must be fully developed. Weak breathing and failure to properly focus the voice are the most frequent causes of singing off the key. They are much more common and mischievous than lack of "ear."

Dr. May tested the breathing of 85 persons, most of them Indians, and found that 79 out of the 85 used abdominal breathing. The chest breathers were from classes "civilized" and more or less "cultured."

Nature has provided that for quiet breathing when at rest the air shall pass through the nose. But when a person is taking active exercise, and consequently demands more air, he naturally and of necessity opens the mouth so as to breathe more fully. While speaking or singing the air is necessarily taken in through the mouth.

BREATH CONTROL

Firmness of tone depends upon steadiness of breath pressure. Steadiness of tone depends upon a control of the breath which allows a minimum volume of air to pass out under sufficient tension to produce vocalization.

The tension and flow of breath can be gradually lessened until the tone vanishes and not even a whisper remains.[Pg 27]

Power and largeness of tone depend first upon the **right use of the resonant cavities**, and second upon the **volume of breath used under proper control**.

In producing high tones the breath is delivered in less amount than for the low tones, but under greater tension. Absolute control of the breath is necessary to produce the best results of which a voice is capable. Full control of the breath insures success to a good voice; without it the best voice is doomed to failure.

When muscular action is fully mastered, and the proper method of breathing understood and established, the muscles of inspiration and expiration will act one against the other, so that the act of breathing may be suspended at any moment, whether the lungs are full, or partly full, or empty. This is muscular control of the breath. Correct breathing is health giving and strength giving; it promotes nutrition, lessens the amount of adipose tissue, and reinforces every physical requisite essential to speaking and singing.

A CURE FOR NERVOUSNESS

It cannot be too widely advertised that the surest remedy for that torture of singers and speakers, nervousness, is the great tranquillizer,—quiet, deep breathing, deeply controlled. The breath of nervousness is quick, irregular, and shallow, therefore, take a few, slow, deliberate, deep, and *rhythmic* inhalations of pure air through the nostrils, and the panting gasp of agitation will vanish. As a help toward deepening the breath and overcoming the spasmodic, clavicular habit, inhale quietly and slowly through the nose, or slowly sip the air through the nearly closed lips as if you were sipping the inmost breath of life itself.

NECESSITY OF BREATHING EXERCISES

To acquire control of breathing, proper exercises must be intelligently and persistently followed. In mankind, nature seems to have been diverted from her normal course so that[Pg 28] we seldom find an individual who breathes correctly without education in the matter. What we have said on breathing is based on the premise that respiration involves coördinate action of the body from collar-bone to the base of the abdomen; that is, expanding and contracting the chest and abdomen simultaneously. This is called "lateral-abdominal" breathing; as the chest is the thoracic cavity, "abdomino-thoracic" has been suggested as brief and more strictly scientific.

Work on any other lines fails to develop the full power and quality of the voice. Weak breathing is a prime cause of throaty tones. In such cases an effort is made to increase the tone by pinching the larynx. But this compresses the vocal cords, increases the resistance to the passage of the breath, and brings rigidities that prevent proper resonance. The true way is to increase the wind supply, as does the organist.

CORRECT BREATHING ILLUSTRATED

The following figures show the outline of correct breathing. The inner abdominal line shows the limit of expiration; the outer line shows the limit of full inspiration.

Figure 9 shows the limit of full expiration and inspiration of the male, side view.

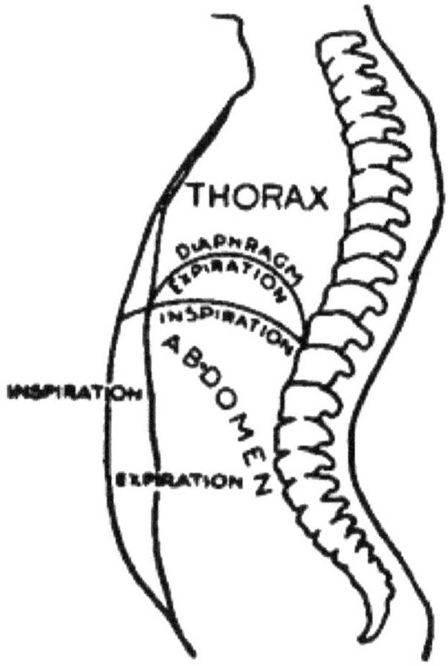

FIGURE 9.

Figure 10 shows the lateral expansion of the ribs in both expiration and inspiration, front view of the male.

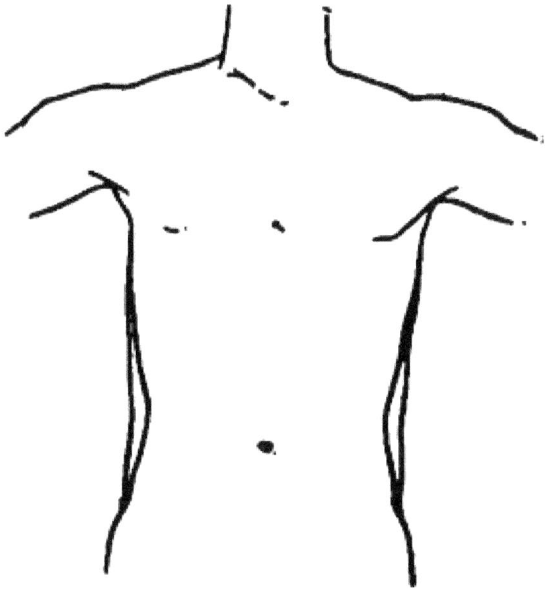

FIGURE 10.

The expansion cannot be great at this part of the chest, as the side is so short a distance from the backbone to which the ribs are attached. The movement of the ribs in front is much greater, as Fig. 9 shows.

Figure 11 shows the front expansion and contraction in the breathing of the female, side view.

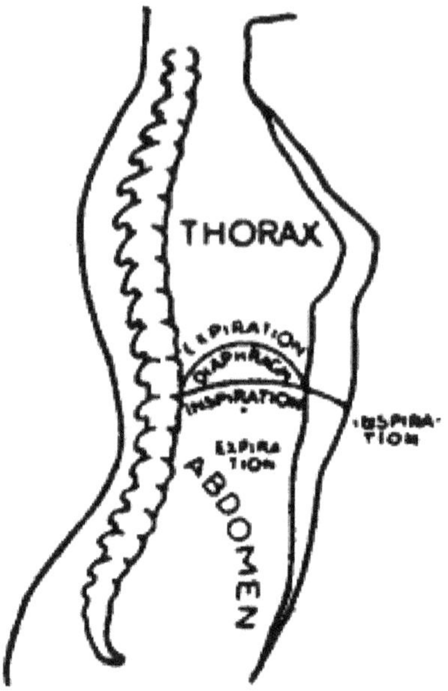

FIGURE 11.

Figure 12 shows the lateral expansion of the chest in the female, front view.

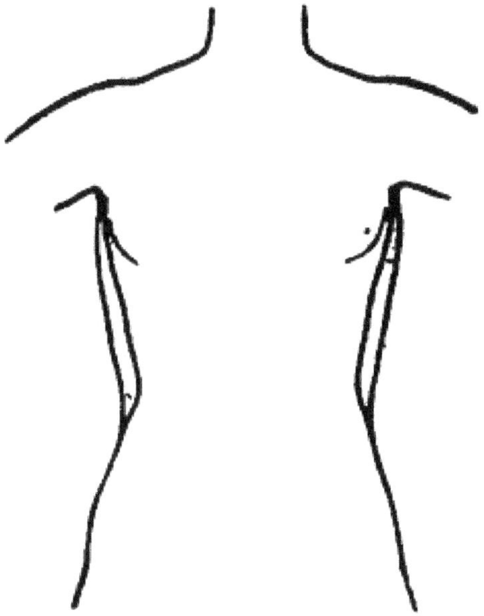

FIGURE 12.

These diagrams are made from photographs, and thus true to life. It will be noticed that there is no difference in the breathing outline between these subjects. The female subject, though a good singer, had had no training in breathing.[Pg 29] She previously insisted that she used only the chest breathing, and did not use the abdominal muscles, but actual test revealed the condition to be that shown in Figure 11 and convinced her that she was mistaken.

It is not unlikely that many other singers who now think they are using only the high chest respiration would, if subjected to the same test, find themselves similarly mistaken.

The contraction incident to forced expiration is much more tense than the enlargement of forced inspiration. When singing or speaking, forced inspiration is not used. Experience shows that the change in size of the body during speaking or singing is usually small. Occasionally, long passages in music demand that the expulsive power of the breathing apparatus be used to its limit.

ECONOMY OF BREATH

The quantity of air taken in with a single inspiration is, in quiet breathing, according to Prof. Mills,[3] from twenty to thirty cubic inches, but this may be increased in the deepest inspiration to about one hundred cubic inches. In forcible expiration about one hundred cubic inches may be expelled, but even then the residual air that cannot be expelled is about one hundred cubic inches.

It is not, however, the quantity of breath inhaled that is significant, it is the amount *controlled*. Get, therefore, all the breath necessary, and keep it, but without undue effort and *without rigidity*.

To test the amount of breath used in prolonged vocalization, a person skilled in the art of breathing, after an ordinary inspiration, closed his lips, stopped his nostrils, and began to vocalize. He found that the mouth with distended cheeks held sufficient breath to continue a substantial tone for twenty-three seconds.

While these experiments show that very little amount or force of breath is needed to produce effective tones, the impression must exist in the mind of the performer that there is a free flow of breath through the larynx; otherwise the tone will seem restricted and will be weak. The forced holding back of the breath begets a restraint that has a bad effect on the singer's delivery. While the breath must be controlled, there is such a thing as an exaggerated "breath control" that makes free delivery of the voice impossible.

It is quite possible to *overcrowd* the lungs with air. Do not, therefore, make the mistake of always taking the largest possible breath. Reserve this for the climaxes, and inhale according to the requirements of the phrase and its dynamics. The constant taking of too much breath is a common mistake, but trying to sing too long on one breath is another.

THE INITIAL USE OF BREATH FORCE

The breath force when properly employed seems to be expended in starting the vibrations in the larynx; the vibrations are then transmitted to the air in the resonance cavities, and there the perfected tone sets the outer air in motion, through which the tone vibrations are conveyed to the ear of the listener.

RESERVE BREATH POWER

The correctly trained singer or speaker will never allow the breath power to be exhausted. Some breath should be taken in at every convenient interval between the words, according to the punctuation, but never between syllables of a word;, this is correct phrasing. In this way the lungs are kept nearly full, and breathing is at its best.

The chief cause of breath exhaustion is *wasted* breath. This waste comes from exhaling more breath (more motive power) than the tone requires, and *breath that does not become tone is wasted.* This fault is largely induced by lack of proper resonance adjustment.

The singer should always feel able to sing another note or to speak another word. To sing or speak thirty or forty counts with one breath is useful practice but poor performance. Occasionally, long runs in singing may compel an exception. Half-empty lungs lower the pitch of the tone, lessen the resonance, and weaken the voice, rendering the last note of the song and the last word of the sentence inaudible. The breathing must not be forced, but enough air must be furnished to produce the proper full vibrations.[Pg 32]

What then does perfect control of the breath mean?

1. Ability to fill the lungs to their capacity either quickly or slowly.

2. Ability to breathe out as quickly or slowly as the occasion demands.

3. Ability to suspend inspiration, with the throat open, whether the lungs are full or not, and to resume the process at will without having lost any of the already inspired air.

4. Ability to exhale under the same restrictions.

The above four points are common to speaking and singing, but singing involves further:

5. Ability to sing and sustain the voice on an *ordinary* breath.

6. Ability to *quietly* breathe as often as text and phrase permit.

7. Ability to breathe so that the fullest inspiration *brings no fatigue*.

8. Ability to so economize the breath that the *reserve is never exhausted*.

9. The ability to breathe so naturally, so unobtrusively, that *neither breath nor lack of breath is ever suggested to the listener*—this is the very perfection of the art.

CHAPTER IV
BREATHING EXERCISES

ENOUGH has been said in the preceding chapter to make clear the necessity of breath control, and to show what constitutes this control for the singer—the professional breather.

If the singer's breathing is nothing but an amplification of normal, healthy breathing, why dwell upon it, why not let it develop of itself?

Unfortunately, many teachers have taken this attitude, overlooking the fact that, although life is dependent on normal, healthy breathing, such breathing is, in civilized communities, not the rule but the exception, simply because normal living is rare; the artificiality of modern life forbids it. The high pressure under which most people live induces mental tension together with the consequent nervous and muscular tension. We are, without being conscious of it, so habituated to unnatural tension that automatic breathing is shallow and irregular instead of being deep and rhythmic.

The task, therefore, is to reclaim a neglected birthright—natural breathing—to make it habitual and amplify it.

PRELIMINARY SUGGESTIONS

1. Breathing exercises to be invigorating and purifying demand plenty of fresh air.

2. At first do not practise longer than ten minutes at a time, three times a day.

3. Gradually lengthen the time without overdoing. When tired stop.

4. The best time is before dressing in the morning, with the window open. The worst time is directly after a meal.

5. Maintain throughout an easy, flexible poise.

6. Breathe as *deeply* as possible without abdominal disten[Pg 34]tion. The greatest expansion should be felt at the lower end of the breast-bone.

7. Breathe as *broadly* as possible, expanding the sides without tension.

8. Breathe as *high* as possible without shoulder movement or stiffness.

9. Use not the high breath alone, or the mid-breath, or the low breath, but use the *complete* breath.

10. Breathe *rhythmically* by counting mentally.

11. Breathe *thoughtfully* rather than mechanically.

12. Do not crowd the lungs or lay stress on the mere quantity of air you can inhale. The intake of breath is, for the singer, secondary to its control, economy, and application in song. Increase of lung capacity will duly appear.

13. When not singing, speaking or practising an exercise that demands it, *keep your mouth shut*.

ATTITUDE

Dress the neck and body loosely, so as to give the throat and trunk perfect freedom. Place the hands on the hips, so as to free the chest from the weight of the arms. Stand erect, evenly upon the balls of the feet; the body straight, but not strained. Raise the back of the head slightly without bending the neck.

This action will straighten the spine, place the chest forward, and bring the abdomen backward into its proper relation.

The great majority of people are shallow breathers, chest breathers, who when told to take a "deep breath" do not know what is meant. It is therefore necessary for them first to learn what a deep breath is, and then how to take it.

Exercise I

FOR THOSE WHO DO NOT KNOW WHAT A DEEP BREATH IS

Before rising in the morning, remove your pillow and while flat on your back place one hand lightly on the abdomen, the other on the lower ribs. Relax the whole body, giving up your[Pg 35] whole weight to the bed. Inhale through the nostrils slowly, evenly, and deeply, while mentally counting one, two, three, four, etc. As you inhale, notice (*a*) the gradual expansion of the abdomen, (*b*) the side expansion of the lower ribs, (*c*) the rise and inflation of the chest, without raising the shoulders. Hold the breath while mentally counting four (four seconds), then suddenly let the breath go, and notice the collapse of the abdomen and lower chest. Remember *the inspiration must be slow and deep, the expiration sudden and complete.* Practise this preliminary exercise for not more than ten minutes each morning for a week. The second week hold the breath six seconds, instead of four, and gradually increase the time, without overdoing.

While, for a novice, the exercises may be taken at first in bed, this is but a preliminary to their practise standing in easy poise as directed in the preceding section.

Exercise II

SLOW INHALATION WITH SUDDEN EXPULSION

Inhale as in I; hold the breath four counts (seconds) or more; then expel the air vigorously in one breath through the wide open mouth. The beginner is often helped in acquiring a deep breath by slowly sipping breath. Therefore as a variant to Exercise II practise:

Exercise III

SIPPING THE BREATH, WITH QUICK EXHALATION

Through the smallest possible opening of the lips, while mentally counting, inhale very slowly and steadily; hold two to four counts, then expel the air all at once through the wide open mouth.

Exercise IV

FOR RIB EXPANSION

To more completely arouse dormant muscles that should play an important part in breathing, place the hands against the sides, thumbs well back, take, through the nostrils or[Pg 36] the slightly parted lips, six short catch-breaths, moving the ribs *out at the side* with each catch-breath. Hold the breath two counts, and exhale through the mouth with six short expiratory puffs, drawing the ribs *in at the side* with each puff.

Exercise V

SLOW INHALATION WITH SLOW EXPIRATION

Inhale as in I, while mentally counting one, two, three, four, etc., until the inhalation seems complete. Hold the breath four or more counts; then exhale through the nostrils slowly and evenly while mentally counting to the number reached in the inspiration. With practice the number of counts will gradually increase. Do not, however, force the increase. The muscles that control inspiration are powerful; do not, therefore, make the mistake of seeking to control expiration by contraction of the glottis. Practise these exercises with an open throat and depend on the breathing muscles for control of the outgoing air. Remember that *singing is control of breath in exit*.

Exercise VI

RAPID INSPIRATION WITH SLOW EXPIRATION

Inhale through the nostrils quickly, deeply, and forcefully (one count); hold two counts; exhale through the nostrils evenly, steadily, and as slowly as possible while mentally counting one, two, three, four, etc. With practice gradually increase the number of counts for the exhalation.

Exercise VII

FARINELLI'S GREAT EXERCISE

The Cavalier, Don Carlo Broschi, better known as Farinelli (1705-1782), the world's greatest singer in bravura and coloratura, was a pupil of Porpora and Bernacchi. There was no branch of the art which he did not carry to the highest perfection, and the successes of his youth did not prevent him from continuing his study, or, when his name was famous, from[Pg 37] acquiring by much perseverance another style and a superior method. His breath control was considered so marvelous in that day of great singers, it is said, that the art of taking and keeping the breath so softly and easily that no one could perceive it began and died with him. He is said to have spent several hours daily in practising the following exercise:

As in Exercise III, sip the breath slowly and steadily through the smallest possible opening of the lips; hold it a few counts, then exhale very slowly and steadily through the smallest possible opening of the lips.

Farinelli's exercise is not for beginners.

Exercise VIII

THE CLEANSING BREATH

For ventilating and sweeping the lungs, for quick refreshment after fatigue, and for use always at the close of your exercises, inhale through the nostrils slowly a complete breath; hold two to four counts, purse the lips tightly and expel through them a small puff of air, hold two counts, puff one, hold two counts, puff one, and so on until the exhalation is complete. A few trials should convince you that this simple exercise is of great value.

HALF-BREATH

In both singing and speaking, the sustained delivery of long phrases or sentences sometimes makes unusual demands on the breath supply. It is a law of good singing that every phrase should end with the breath unexhausted. When the flow of text and music forbid the taking of a full breath, half-breaths must be quietly taken at convenient points. Instead of letting the whole reservoir of motive power exhaust itself and then completely refill it, we should, by taking these half-breaths, maintain a reserve. A notable advocate of the use of the half-breath in singing is that past mistress of sustained and smooth delivery, Marcella Sembrich.

CHAPTER V
REGISTERS

THE subject of registers has always been the *bête noire* of vocalists, a source of controversy and confusion. The term "register," as commonly used, means a series of tones of a characteristic clang or quality, produced by the same mechanism. The term "break" is generally used to indicate the point at which a new register with sudden change appears.

The advocates of registers lay stress either on the changes in laryngeal action, or the changes in tone quality. Before the days of the laryngoscope, registers were treated simply as different qualities of tone, characterizing a certain portion of the voice's compass.

Those who encourage the cultivation of register consciousness claim to do so for the sake of the differences in tone-color which they associate with the different "registers." The purpose of the following chapters is to show that the quality or color of a tone is altogether a matter of resonance, and *not* a question of laryngeal action.

Moreover, the mechanism of the larynx is not voluntary in its action, but automatic, and even if a singer knew how the vocal cords should act it would not help him in the least to govern their action. The fact is that the results of laryngoscopic study of the vocal cords have been disappointing and contradictory and investigators have failed to define what correct laryngeal action is. There are those who even deny that the vocal cords govern the pitch of the voice.

In her thoughtful *Philosophy of Singing*, Clara Kathleen Rogers, while upholding "registers," says that considered physiologically "the different registers of the voice should be regarded by the singer as only so many *modifications in*[Pg 39] *the quality of tone*, which modifications are inherent in the voice itself." She then adds significantly: "These modifications are not brought about by conscious adjustments of the parts employed, as any interference with the parts will produce that obstacle to quality we call a 'break.'"

One of the greatest of modern singers, Mme. Lilli Lehmann, in her interesting work, *How to Sing*, says: "Do registers exist by nature? No. It may be said that they are created through long years of speaking in the vocal range that is easiest to the person, or in one adopted by imitation." She speaks of three ranges of the voice, or, rather, three sections of the vocal range, as chest, middle, and head, saying, "All three form registers *when exaggerated*." After speaking of the hopeless confusion that results from clinging to the appellations of chest, middle, and head *register*, confounding voice with register, she concludes:

"As long as the word 'register' is kept in use the registers will not disappear, and yet the register question must be swept away, to give place to another class of ideas, sounder views on the part of teachers, and a truer conception on the part of singers and pupils."

The trend of recent thought on this subject is further shown in Ffrangcon-Davies' important work, *The Singing of the Future*, where, having in mind "the useless torture to which thousands of students have been subjected," he characterizes "breaks" and "registers" as "paraphernalia supplied by credulity to charlatanism"; and adds: "How many a poor pupil has become a practical monomaniac on the subject of *that break in my voice between D and D sharp*!"

My own studies convince me that there is but one register, or, rather, no such thing as register, save as it applies to the compass of the voice; and that chest, middle, head, and all other registers are creations of false education. Training based upon the theory of many registers results in an artificial and unnatural division of the voice.[Pg 40]

THE VOICE AND INSTRUMENTS COMPARED

The organ of the voice has long been considered the analogue of every other instrument except in regard to registers. Investigation indicates that it is analogous in this respect also. Compare the voice instrument with the pianoforte, violin, and organ and the similarity will plainly appear. The artificial instruments undergo no change when making a tone of higher or lower pitch other than the attuning of the vibrator to the pitch desired. All other parts remain the same. So when the voice is correctly focused and delivered, the only change incident to altered pitch is that made in the vibrator so as to give the proper number of vibrations for the pitch required. If the scale is sung down, using the same vowel sound for the whole scale, the comparison will be appreciated; the pupil will not be conscious of any change in the vocal organ or experience any difficulty in descending the scale. Faithful advocates of the theory of many registers say: "Whenever in doubt about the production of a tone, sing *down* to it from some tone above it, never *upward* from a tone below," for they find that singing down "blends the registers." This we believe is because in singing down muscular and nerve tension is gradually relaxed and consequently there is no "register" change in the voice.

A study of the church organ will, I think, make this matter clear. The organ has many so-called registers, as the *vox humana*, *flute*, *oboe*, etc. These differ in the character of tone produced, because of the size and shape of the different sets of pipes and the material, wood or metal, of which they are made. But each similarly constructed set of pipes forms only one register, and the pitch of the set varies from low to high without any abrupt change in quality. All the tones are produced by the same methods and means, the bellows, the vibrator, and the pipe. In length and diameter, the pipe is proper to the tone produced: a short pipe of small diameter for the high tones, and a long, wide pipe for the bass tones.

The short vibrations of the high tones are perceived by the ear as affecting the air only, while the tones of the lowest bass[Pg 41] pipes shake the solid foundations as well as the superstructure. So with the human voice. The coarser tissues cannot answer to the short vibrations of the upper tones, because they cannot move so quickly, while they can, and do, respond to the vibrations of the low tones. This may cause some difference in degree, but not in kind. With all tones focused alike, the low tones of the human organ may be regarded as head tones plus the vibrations of the coarser tissues.

It has been said of registers that they are "acoustic illusions which disappear in the perfectly trained voice." As soon as the singer has learned to use his voice normally all these defective changes disappear.

TWO CASES

The following incident illustrates the fact that registers are an artificial creation: A young lady who had been a patient of the author since her childhood studied elocution in a metropolitan city, and to improve her voice took vocal music lessons of a teacher of more than local repute. He found no end of trouble in teaching her to "blend the registers," and she had utterly failed to acquire the art. One summer she came back for professional services and told her troubles. During the few weeks of her stay she followed the author's suggestions, and was fully convinced of their correctness and efficiency. Upon returning to her lessons, she followed, without any explanations, the method that had been outlined for her. Her success in "blending the registers" was a surprise to her teacher who heartily congratulated her upon what she had accomplished during the summer.

Another case is that of a young lady who was under the author's direction as to vocal culture from childhood. As early as four years of age she was taught by the use of a few exercises to focus the voice in the nose and head, and to recognize the head vibrations by a light touch of the finger. When about seven years old, she took ten lessons of a teacher on the same lines, and at fifteen years of age took another brief[Pg 42] course. In the meantime she had only the practice obtained by singing with the pupils in the schools she attended. Later, of her own volition, she sang more, and carefully applied the principles she had been taught, with the result that her voice compassed nearly two octaves, evenly and smoothly, with no break or change of focus or quality, or other intimation of "register," and she developed a speaking voice of more than ordinary quality and resonance.

It has also been my lot to aid in the development of the voices of many patients after a surgical operation for cleft palate. Success has proven the correctness and efficacy of the principles set forth in these pages.

A majority of the more than fifty authors whose works I have examined have laid great stress on the distinction between head and chest tones, open and closed tones, pure and impure tones, have warned against the nasal tone, and have constantly advocated a natural tone. That there is no essential difference between a head tone and a chest tone has already been discussed and, it would seem, conclusively proven. Any tone, closed or open, is pure and musical if properly focused and delivered, and the singer is at liberty to use either upon any note of the scale if it will serve better to express the sentiment he wishes to convey to the hearer. The cooing of the love song, the cry of alarm for help, and the shout of the military charge require very different qualities of voice to express the feelings, yet each may be musical and will be so if properly delivered.

CHAPTER VI

RESONANCE IN GENERAL

THE intimate relationship existing between voice culture and the science of acoustics was formerly slightly perceived. The teaching of singing, as an art, then rested altogether on an empirical basis, and the acoustics of singing had not received the attention of scientists.

With the publication in 1863 of Helmholtz's great work[4] a new era began, although singer and scientist yet continue to look upon each other with suspicion. Teachers of the voice, casting about for a scientific basis for their work, were greatly impressed with Helmholtz's revelations in regard to vocal resonance—the fact that tones are modified in quality as well as increased in power by the resonance of the air in the cavities of pharynx and head.

Writing in 1886, Edmund J. Meyer speaks of the importance of a "study of the influence of the different resonance cavities as the voice is colored by one or the other, and the tuning each to each and each to all"; yet, he adds, "the subject is seldom heard of outside of books."

The basic importance of resonance in the use of the voice is still too little recognized, though obvious enough in the construction of musical instruments. With the exception of a few instruments of percussion, all musical instruments possess three elements,—a *motor*, a *vibrator*, and a *resonator*. The violin has the moving bow for a motor, the strings for a vibrator, and the hollow body for a resonator. The French horn has the lungs of the performer for a motor, the lips for a vibrator, and the gradually enlarging tube, terminating in[Pg 44] the flaring bell, for a resonator. In the pianoforte the hammer-stroke, the strings, and the sounding-board perform the corresponding offices. Though improvements in other parts of the piano have done much to increase the volume of the tone, yet in the radical change of form, size, and other physical qualities of the sounding-board consists the evolution of the modern pianoforte from the primitive clavichord.

In all these instruments the quality and power of the tone depend upon the presence of these three elements,—the perfection of their construction, their proper relation as to size and position, and the perfect adaptation of each part. A split sounding-board spoils the pianoforte, the indented bell destroys the sweet tone of the French horn, and a cracked fiddle is the synonym for pandemonium itself.

The quality and power of resonance is well illustrated by a tuning-fork, which, if set in vibration, can, unaided, scarcely be heard by the person holding it. But if rested on a table, or a plate of glass, or, better still, on the bridge of a violin, its tones may be distinctly heard throughout a large hall.

The vibrating violin string when detached from the body of this instrument, although attuned to pitch, gives absolutely no musical sound; the lips of the player placed on the mouthpiece detached from the tube and bell of the brass instrument produce only a splutter; and a pianoforte without a sounding-board is nil. The air column in the tube of the French horn, and the sounding-board of the pianoforte develop the vibrations caused by the lips and strings into musical tones pleasing to the ear. The tuning-fork alone can scarcely be heard, while the induced vibrations it sets up through properly adjusted resonance may be audible far away.

The vocal cords alone cannot make music any more than can the lips of the cornet player apart from his instrument. *The tone produced by the vibrations alone of the two very small vocal bands must, in the nature of things, be very feeble.*

Ninety-and-nine persons if asked the question, what produces tone in the human-voice, would reply, "the vibrations[Pg 45] of the vocal cords," and stop there, as if that were all; whereas the answer is very incomplete—not even half an answer.

A great deal of the irrational and injurious "teaching" of singing that prevails everywhere, and of the controversy that befogs the subject, is due to the widely prevalent notion that the little vocal cords are the principal cause of tone, whereas they are in themselves insignificant as sound producers.

It is the vibrations of the air in the resonance chambers of the human instrument, together with the induced vibrations of the instrument itself, which give tone its sonority, its reach, its color, and emotional power.

That this is not an empirical statement but a scientific fact, a few simple experiments will demonstrate.

Tone, in the musical sense, is the result of rapid periodic vibration. The pitch of tone depends upon the *number* of vibrations in a given period; the loudness of tone depends upon the *amplitude* of the vibrations; the quality of tone depends upon the *form* of the vibrations; and the form of the vibrations depends upon the *resonator*.

The fact that pure white light is a compound of all the tints of the rainbow into which it may be resolved by the prism is well known, but the analogous fact that a pure musical tone is a compound of tones of different rates of vibration, tones of different pitch, is not so much a matter of common knowledge, and not so obvious.

Analysis shows that a musical tone consists of a fundamental note and a series of overtones.[5] The ear is quite capable of recognizing many of these overtones and may be trained to do so. The most obvious can be readily separated from a fundamental by a simple experiment.

The overtones arrange themselves in a definite order, as follows: (1) the fundamental or prime tone; (2) an overtone one octave above the fundamental; (3) an overtone a fifth[Pg 46] above No. 2; (4) an overtone a fourth above No. 3 (two octaves above the fundamental); (5) an overtone a major third above No. 4; (6) an overtone a minor third above No. 5. There are others in still higher range but those indicated are easily demonstrated on the piano. For C they would be as follows:

[Listen]

Experiment I

Step to your piano, noiselessly press and hold down the key of No. 2, then strike the fundamental No. 1, with force and immediately release it. As a result No. 2 will sound clearly, and if your ears are keen you will at the same time hear No. 6. In succession hold down the keys of 3, 4, 5, and 6, while you strike and release the fundamental No. 1. If your piano is "in tune" you will probably hear No. 6 when holding the key of any other note of the series.

In a musical tone of rich quality the overtones just indicated are present in their fulness, while tone that is weak and thin is made so by the absence or weakness of the overtones. I have stated that the quality of a tone depends on the *form* of its vibrations, and that the form of its vibrations is determined by the character of the *resonator*. We can now amplify this by saying that while the relative presence or absence of overtones determines the clang or color of a tone, their presence or absence is determined by the *character of the resonance.*

An English writer records that he was once in the garden at the back of a house while a gentleman was singing in the drawing-room. The tone-quality was good, and the pitch so unusually high he hastened to learn who sang tenor high C so beautifully. On entering the room, instead of the tenor he had supposed, he found the singer was a baritone, and the note sung was only middle C. The fundamental tone had not[Pg 47] reached him in the garden but the first overtone, an octave above it, had. Concrete illustrations will make the subject still clearer.

Experiment II

If an ordinary tuning-fork when vibrating is held in the hand its intrinsic tone is too weak to carry far. Rest the handle of the vibrating fork on a bare table or the panel of the door, and the sound is greatly augmented. *The vibrations of the fork have by contact induced similar vibrations in the wooden table or panel which reinforce the primary tone.*

Experiment III

Place the handle of the vibrating tuning-fork on a small upturned empty box, or, better still, in contact with the body of a violin, and the sound will be stronger than in the previous experiment, because to the vibrations of the wood are added the vibrations of the air enclosed in the box or the violin. *To the resonance of the wood has been added the sympathetic resonance of the confined air.*

Experiment IV

Hold the vibrating fork over the mouth of an empty fruit-jar and there will probably be little or no reinforcement; but gently pour in water, thereby shortening the air column within the jar, and the sound of the fork will be gradually intensified until at a certain point it becomes quite loud. If you pour in still more water the sound will gradually become feebler. This shows that *for every tone an air column of a certain size most powerfully reinforces that tone.*

Experiment V

As a sequence to the last experiment, take two fruit-jars of the same size, and, having learned to what point to fill them for the greatest resonance, fill one jar (after warming it) to the required point with hot water, the other with cold water,[Pg 48] and you will find that the resonance of the heated, therefore expanded, air is much less than the denser air of the cold jar. This shows that *the degree of density of the air affects its resonance.*

Experiment VI

To demonstrate the resonance of the oral cavity, apart from the voice, hold a vibrating tuning-fork before the open mouth. Vary the shape and size of the cavity until the sound of the fork suddenly increases in volume, showing that the right adjustment for resonance has been made. *This intensification of the sound is due to the vibration of the air in the mouth cavity, together with the sympathetic vibration of the surrounding walls.*

Experiment VII

As an illustration of sympathetic resonance without contact, sing forcibly a tone that is within easy range, and at the same time silently hold down the corresponding key of the piano. On ceasing to sing you will hear the tone sounding in the piano. This may be further illustrated by playing on the open string of one violin while another, tuned to the same pitch, rests untouched near by. Through *sympathetic resonance* the corresponding string of the second violin will vibrate and sound its note. The louder the first violin is played the louder will be the sympathetic tone of the second.

The deep pedal-tones of a church organ often induce sympathetic resonance that may be felt beneath the feet of the listener. One writer, a singer, speaks of living in the same house with two deaf-mutes. He lodged on the first floor, they on the third. One day, meeting at luncheon, one of the deaf-mutes told the singer that he had begun practice earlier that morning than usual. Surprised, the writer asked how he knew. The deaf-mute replied that they always knew when he was singing because they felt the floor of their room vibrate.

If tone vibrations can be transmitted so readily throughout[Pg 49] a house, it is not difficult to understand how easily the vibrations of bone and tissue can be transmitted until the whole framework of the body responds in perceptible vibration.

It is said that Pascal at the age of twelve wrote a dissertation on acoustics suggested by his childish discovery that when a metal dish was struck by a knife the resulting sound could be stopped by touching the vibrating dish with a finger.

With this in mind it is not difficult to understand how compression of the human instrument by the pressure of tight clothing without, or by false muscular tension within, must interfere with its free vibration and so rob the produced tone of just so much of perfection.

From these experiments we can understand that, while the tones of the voice are initiated by or at the vocal cords, the volume and character of the tones are dependent upon *resonance,*—the vibration of the air in the various resonance chambers of the body, together with the sympathetic vibration of the walls of these chambers and the bony framework that supports them.

In respect to resonance, as in other respects, the human voice is far superior to all other instruments, for their resonators are fixed and unchanging, while the human resonator is flexible,—in Helmholtz's words "admits of much variety of form, so that many more qualities of tone can be thus produced than on any instrument of artificial construction."

We are now prepared to realize the error of the common notion that loudness of tone is due entirely to increase of breath pressure on the vocal cords. Simple experiments with the tuning-fork have shown that while the volume of sound it gives forth is due in part to the amplitude of its vibrations, its loudness is *chiefly* due to the character of the *resonance* provided for it.

The larger the resonance chamber the greater is its reinforcing capacity. The largest air chamber in the body is the chest, which serves not only as a wind-chest, but as a resonance chamber. The necessity for chest expansion, therefore,[Pg 50] is not, as generally supposed, merely for air, but to increase its size as a resonance chamber.

In view of the laws of tone, how great is the common error of speaking of the larynx as if it alone were the vocal organ, when the principal vibrations are *above* the vocal cords in the chambers of *resonance*!

Since the musical value, the beauty of tone, as well as its volume, comes only from right use of the resonator, our principal business must be the acquiring control of the vibratory air current *above the larynx*. The acquirement of this control involves the proper focusing or placing of the tone, with the free uncramped use of all the vocal organs; power will then take care of itself.

CHAPTER VII
HEAD AND NASAL RESONANCE

OF the four component factors in the production of speech and song, the first, the *motor*, has been considered in Chapter III, and the second, the *vibrator*, in Chapter I.

In one respect there is marked contrast between these two factors. Until right habits are so thoroughly formed that the singer's breathing is automatically controlled, conscious effort is necessary, while the action of the vibrator, the vocal cords, is involuntary, not subject to conscious control.

The subtle adjustments of the delicate mechanism of the larynx belong to the realm of reflex action—to a spontaneous activity that, left unhindered, does its part in perfect nicety.

The vocal cords must, in their action, be free from the disturbance of uncontrolled breath action below them, or the hindrance due to misdirected effort above them. To direct consciousness to the vocal cords is to cramp them and prevent that free vibration and that perfect relaxation of the throat without which pure tone and true pitch are impossible.

As a surgeon I well know the value of thorough anatomical knowledge, but from the singer's standpoint I cannot too strongly emphasize the unwisdom of directing the attention of sensitively organized pupils to their vocal mechanism by means of the laryngoscope. This instrument belongs to the physician, not to the singer.

The importance of the third factor, the *resonator*, has been considered in Chapter V, on Resonance, but the fourth element in voice production, *articulation*, is so coördinated to resonance that the significance and primacy of the latter are too often overlooked.

Placing or "focusing the voice" I have found to be chiefly[Pg 52] a matter of control and use of the resonator, consisting of chest, pharynx, mouth, and the nasal and head cavities.

A tone lacking in resonance is ineffective,—devoid of carrying power,—is diffuse and unfocused; while a resonant tone, no matter how soft dynamically, has carrying power and is focused in its vibration.

Now "voice placing" depends primarily on correct *vowel placing,* which in turn depends on proper adjustment of the resonators, which again depends chiefly on the positions and motions of the organs of articulation. The interdependence of tone quality and pronunciation is therefore obvious.

Constant emphasis must be laid upon the fact that focusing a tone is a matter of resonance, and that perhaps the most important element in this is *nasal* resonance. In this country, particularly, teachers have, in their desire to overcome the too common nasal twang, mistakenly sought to shut out the nasal chamber from all participation in speech and song.

There are those who, partly recognizing the importance of *head* resonance, would secure it while ignoring *nasal* resonance. It is impossible to secure head resonance in this fashion, for it is only through free nasal resonance that the coördinate resonance in the air sinuses above the nasal cavity and connected with it can be established.

The fear of nasal twang and failure to distinguish between it and true nasal resonance has been the stumbling block. They are very different,—one is to be shunned, the other to be cultivated. The first is an obvious blemish, the second is an important essential of good singing.

Nasal tones are caused by a raised or stiffened tongue, a sagging soft palate, a stiffened jaw, or by other rigidities that prevent free tone emission and which at the same time—note this—prevent true nasal resonance.

As tone, or vocalized breath, issues from the larynx, it is divided into two streams or currents by the pendent veil of the soft palate. One stream flows directly into the mouth, where it produces oral resonance; the other stream passes through[Pg 53] the nasopharynx into the hollow chambers of the face and head, inducing nasal and head resonance.

It is commonly supposed that tone passing in whole or in part through the nasal cavities must be nasal in quality; whereas a tone of objectionable nasal quality can be sung equally well with the nostrils either closed or open.

Browne and Behnke state the matter thus: "However tight the closure of the soft palate may be, it is never sufficient to prevent the air in the nasal cavities being thrown into co-vibrations with that in the mouth. These co-vibrations are, in fact, necessary for a certain amount of the brilliancy of the voice, and if they are prevented by a stoppage of the posterior openings of the nasal passages, the voice will sound dull and muffled. This is of course due, to an *absence of nasal resonance*, and must on no account be described as nasal *twang*. It is, indeed, the very opposite of it."

Nasal tone quality and nasal resonance must not be confounded. A nasal tone is constricted, while a tone with nasal resonance is free. Again, a tone may be unmarred by the nasal quality, yet if it lacks nasal resonance it lacks vibrancy, carrying power.

Nasal tones are produced, not because the vibrations pass through the nasal passage, but because they are obstructed in their passage through them. A nasal tone is always a cramped tone, due to impediment, tension, or muscular contraction, particularly in the nasopharynx.

The congestion and consequent thickening of the mucous membrane lining the cavities of the nose and head, resulting from a cold, make the tone muffled and weak, owing to the inability of the parts to respond to the vibrations and add to the tone normal nasal resonance.

The elder Booth (Junius Brutus), about 1838, suffered from a broken nose which defaced his handsome visage and spoiled his splendid voice. His disability was so great that afterward he seldom played. That the cause of this impairment of Booth's voice was due to the contraction and more or less[Pg 54] complete obstruction of the nasal passages is too evident to call for comment.

Many singers have sweet but characterless voices that lack the fulness, power, and ring they might have because they fail to avail themselves of the augmenting power of the resonance cavities. The singer must learn to habitually use all of the resonance cavities and use them simultaneously.

Lilli Lehmann, in *How to Sing*, says that, "although the nasal sound can be exaggerated,—which rarely happens,—it can be much neglected,—something that very often happens." The context makes clear that what in the English translation of the great singer's book is called "nasal sound" is exactly what we term *nasal resonance.*

After charging the monotonous quality or lack of color in the voice of a famous opera star to lack of nasal resonance, Madame Lehmann speaks of the consummate art of Marcella Sembrich who "in recent years appears to have devoted very special study to nasal resonance, whereby her voice, especially in the middle register, has gained greatly in warmth." She says further that nasal resonance "cannot be studied enough. It ought always to be employed." "How often," she says, "have I heard young singers say, 'I no longer have the power to respond to the demands made upon me,' whereas the trouble lies only in the insufficient use of the resonance of the head cavities."

From the foregoing, the conclusion follows that the head vibrations are not only an essential element, but that nasal resonance is a most important element in imparting to tone its brilliance and carrying power. Without thought of the mechanism of *how* nasal resonance is produced, the singer has control over it by direct influence of the will. The tones, low as well as high, should seem to start in the nose and head, and the vibrations of the perfect tone can be plainly felt upon any part of the nose and head. Without the head vibrations no tone can be perfect, for nothing else will compensate for the lack of these. Vocal organs used as here described will[Pg 55] suffer no fatigue from reasonable use; hoarseness will be to them a thing unknown, and "minister's sore throat" an unheard of complaint. Not only is faulty voice production a source of great discomfort, but it is the cause of many diseases of the chest, throat, and head.

The gentle practice in easy range of the exercises given in the chapter following, will do much to restore a normal condition.

CHAPTER VIII

PLACING THE VOICE

WHAT is called "placing the voice" or "tone production" or "focusing the voice" is, as already stated in the previous chapter, chiefly a matter of resonance—of control of the resonator. Now vocalization is largely vowelization, and vocal tones are a complex of sound and resonance. The character of a vowel is given it by the shape of the vowel chamber; and the shaping of the vowel chamber depends upon delicate adjustment of the movable parts,—jaw, lips, cheeks, tongue, veil of the palate, and pharynx. While this adjustment is made through more or less conscious muscular action, the parts must never be forced into position; local effort to this end will invariably defeat itself. The important consideration in all voice movements is a flexible, *natural* action of all the parts, and all the voice movements are so closely allied, so sympathetically related, that if one movement is constrained the others cannot be free. It is a happy fact that *the right way is the easiest way*, and a fundamental truth that **right effort is the result of right thought**. From these axiomatic principles we deduce the very first rule for the singer and speaker,—**THINK the right tone, mentally picture it; then concentrate upon the picture, not upon the mechanism**.

WHEN IS THE VOCAL ACTION CORRECT?

There are two sound criterions for judging the correctness of vocal action,—first, the *ease* of the action, its naturalness, its flexibility. As Mills concisely states it: "He sings or speaks best who attains the end with the least expenditure of energy." Second, the *beauty* of the result. Harsh, unlovely tones are a sure indication of misplaced effort, of tension somewhere,[Pg 57] of wrong action. On the other hand the nearer the tones approach to perfection the closer does the organism come to correct action. *Beauty of tone*, then, is the truest indication of proper vocal action.

Judgment as to the relative beauty of a tone depends on the training of the ear. Pupils should habitually listen to their own voices, for between the hearing and feeling of the voice a knowledge of progress can be obtained. The function of the ear in governing voice production is thus stated by Prof. Mills: "The nervous impulses that pass from the ear to the brain are the most important guides in determining the necessary movements." Mr. Ffrangcon-Davies maintains that, "The training of the ear is one-half of the training of the voice." The student should improve every opportunity to hear the best singers and speakers, for both consciously and unconsciously we learn much by imitation. Good examples are often our best teachers.

Keeping well in mind the principles stated above, we are now ready to begin their application in placing the voice—that is, in setting it free—not by learning some strange and difficult action, but by cultivating normal action.

EXERCISES FOR PRACTICE

The following exercises are designed for the primary development of a correct tone and for the test of the perfection of every tone at every stage of development. They are based upon the assumption that all tones of the voice should be focused and delivered precisely alike. Their use should constitute a part of the daily practice of the singer or speaker.

I give but few exercises for each point to be gained. Intelligent teachers and pupils will add an infinite variety to suit each case, but the exercises given appear to me to be the best for initial practice. It is important that each exercise in its order shall be thoroughly mastered before taking up the next. Only in this way can rapid progress be made, for it is not the multiplicity of exercises, but the thoughtful application of principles in the few, that leads to results.[Pg 58]

The sound of *hng* will always place the voice in proper focus by developing the resonance of the nose and head. The thin bones of the nose will first respond to the sound and after practice the vibrations can be felt on any part of the head and even more distinctly on the low than on the high tones. To attain this, repeat the sound *hung* times without number, prolonging the *ng* sound at least four counts. To insure the proper course of the vowel sounds through the nasal passages, follow *hung* with the vowel *ee,* as this vowel is more easily focused than any other; then with *oo, oh, aw* and *ah.*

Ah is by far the most difficult sound to focus and should never be used for initial practice. Much valuable time has been lost by the custom of using this sound at first. It should come last.

The *h* is chosen to introduce the vowel sound because in the preparation to produce the sound of the letter *h* the epiglottis is wide open and the vocal cords entirely relaxed, and because less change of the tongue is required when the vowel sound follows.

Preliminary Exercise

Practise this softly on any pitch easy for the voice.

[Listen]

Begin the tone quietly on an easy pitch and continue it softly to the end. Later, after these exercises are mastered on one pitch, use every note within the easy compass of the voice. Leave stridency of tone to the locust. It is no part of a perfect tone. It never appeared in the voices of the most famous singers. Those who allowed themselves to use it passed off the stage early in life. Much better results will be obtained by practising without any accompaniment. The sound of the[Pg 59] piano or other instrument distracts the pupil, prevents both pupil and teacher from hearing the voice, and hinders progress.

IMPORTANT DIRECTIONS

The manner in which Exercise I and those that follow is practised is of the utmost importance. Therefore carefully note and apply the following:

1. Fully pronounce the word *hung* (*u* as in *stung*) at once, and prolong the tone, not on the vowel sound but on the *ng* sound. This establishes the proper head and nasal resonance at the very beginning of the exercise.

2. In passing from *ng* to *ee* be very careful not to change the initial focus or lose the sensation of nasal and head resonance. Do not therefore move the lips or the chin. The only change at this point is the slight movement of the tongue required to pronounce *ee*, which must be a pure vowel without a trace of the preceding *g*.

3. In passing from *ee* to *oo*, from *oo* to *oh*, and so on, do so with the least possible movement of lips and chin. *The initial sensation of nasal and head resonance must not be lost.*

4. Each vowel sound must be distinct in enunciation and pure in quality. Avoid blurring one with the other. Give each its true individuality.

5. As jewels of different hue hung on a string, so must this exercise be the stringing of vowels on a continuous stream of sound.

Exercise I

TO ESTABLISH NASAL AND HEAD RESONANCE

This is an exercise for focusing or placing the voice and developing the vibrations of the nasal and head cavities, the most essential parts of the resonant apparatus. If the nostrils are kept fully open, no nasal twang will be heard. The strength of the tone will correspond to the force of the vibrations of the nose and head, which can be plainly felt by resting the finger lightly upon the side of the nose. The vibrations may[Pg 60] eventually be plainly felt on the top and back of the head.

Attack, that is, begin the tone, *softly* and on no account force it in the least. Pronounce the full word *at once*, prolong the *ng* four counts as indicated, and sing the five vowel sounds on a continuous, unbroken tone. Articulate entirely with the lips and without moving the under jaw. In this, as in the following exercises, keep the under jaw relaxed and open the mouth so as to separate the teeth as wide apart as is consistent with the action of the lips. See also the illustrations of proper lip position given at the close of Chapter II.

Practice this exercise on any pitch easy for the voice.

Repeat this many times until the nose and head vibrations are fully recognized and established. After mastery of this exercise is acquired, any words ending in *ng* may be repeated. The word *noon* sung quietly on each note of the voice with the final consonant prolonged will be found helpful.

EXERCISES FOR SPEAKERS

When the placing of the voice is accomplished on the one tone (Exercise I), the speaker can go on with practice in reading and reciting, allowing the voice to change its pitch[Pg 61] at its will, only being careful that all the tones are alike in quality.

A profitable exercise for speakers is to pronounce any word or syllable ending with *ng*, as *ming*, *bing*, *sing*, *ring*, *ting*, and follow it with some familiar lines in a monotone, being sure that the tone is the same and produces the same vibrations in the nose and head.

In the case of a person already a public speaker, this new *régime* may not immediately manifest itself in performance, but gradually the right principles will assume control, and speaking be done with ease and effectiveness. Continual daily practice of exercises should be kept up.

If a speaker has a musical ear and some musical knowledge, he will derive great benefit by following out the practice of the exercises for singers. In no way can the voice for speaking be improved so rapidly or decisively as by musical training.

Exercise II

TO ESTABLISH HEAD AND NASAL RESONANCE

As in Exercise I, sing softly, seeking purity of vowel sounds and quality of tone. Fully pronounce *hung* at once, prolonging the *ng* four counts as indicated. Pass from one vowel to the next with the least possible change in the position of the lips and chin. The stream of sound is to be unbroken, the tone focus unchanged, and the sensation of resonance in the upper chambers continuous.

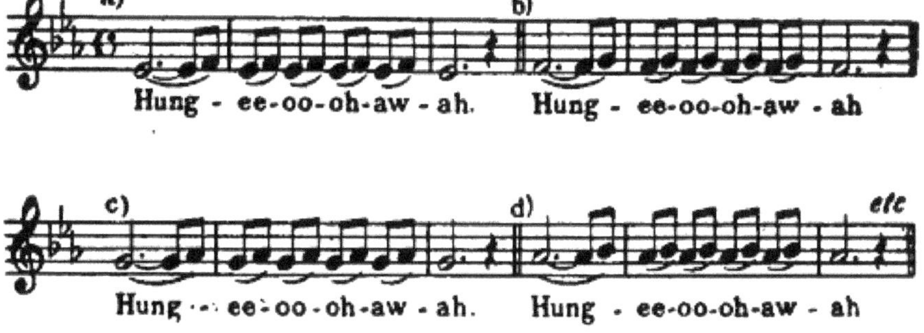

[Pg 62]

Exercise III

UPPER RESONANCE CONTINUED

Follow the directions for Exercise I. Sing quietly in a pitch that is easy for the voice, and modulate up or down by half steps.

Exercise IV

UPPER RESONANCE CONTINUED

The last exercise carried the voice an interval of a third; this carries the voice an interval of a fifth. Follow carefully the directions of Exercise I. Be sure to pronounce *hung* at once, prolonging the tone not on the vowel but on the *ng*. *Sing softly.* Vary the pitch to suit the voice.[Pg 63]

Exercise V

UPPER RESONANCE CONTINUED

The last exercise carried the voice an interval of a fifth, this one has a range of a sixth, while Exercise VI has a range of an octave..

Sing softly in a pitch that is easy for the voice.

Exercise VI

TO ENLARGE THE THROAT AND THUS MAGNIFY THE TONE

Pronounce the word *hung* at once, opening the mouth well. Prolonging the *ng* sound as indicated will insure the proper focus.

Sing the five vowel sounds throughout the scale as indicated. At first practise only on scales that are in easy range.

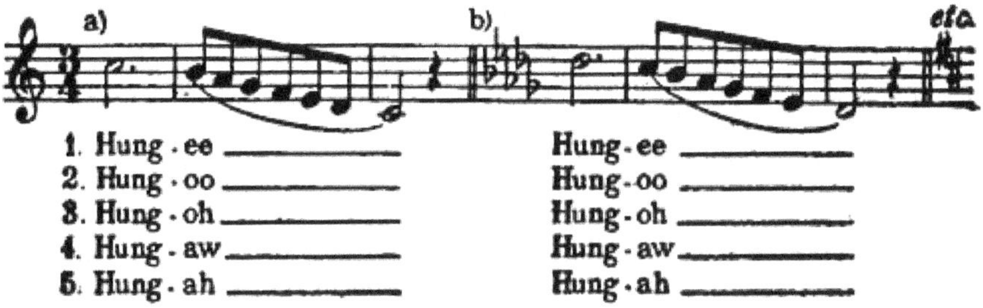

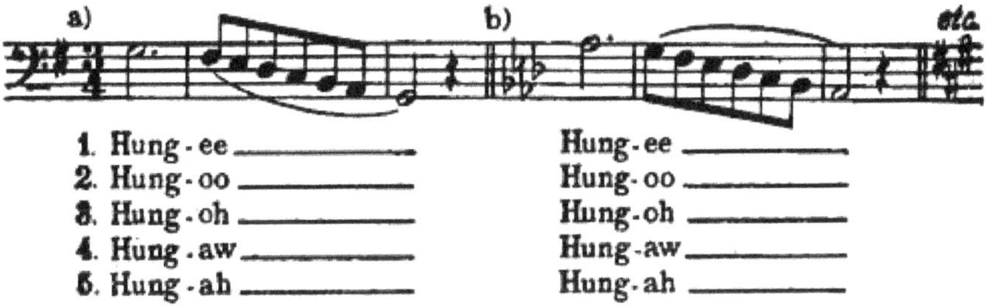

VI[a]

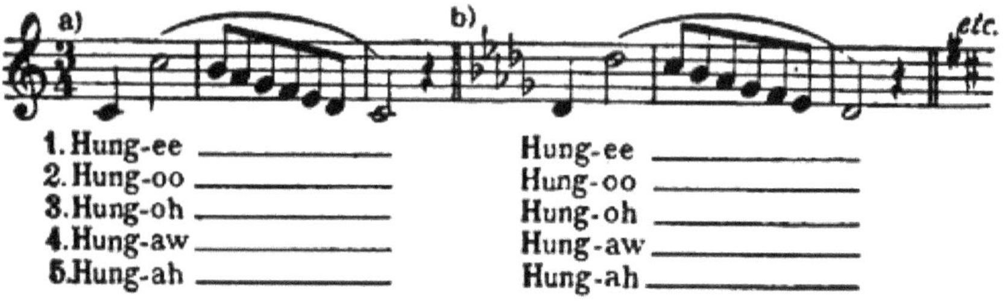

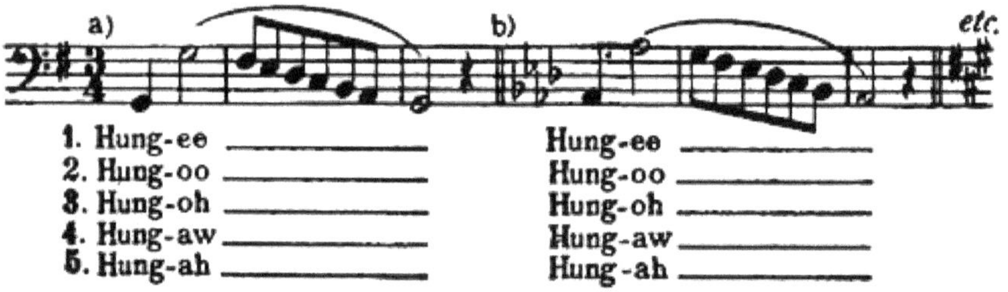

Exercise VII

FOR PRODUCTION OF THE VOWEL SOUNDS IN PROPER FOCUS

Produce the *hung* at once, and add the vowel. *Be sure that the vowel sound follows the same course as the "ng" sound which precedes it, and produces the same sensation in the nose.*

The vowels are arranged in the order chosen because *ee* is the most easily focused while *ah* is by far the most difficult to focus, and hence the worst possible sound for initial practice. *Think* of the tone as being made in the nose and head.

Let there be no break or stopping of the tone when passing from the *ng* sound to the vowel. Simply change the tone into the vowel desired by the proper change in the articulating organs.

Sing the five vowel sounds connectedly, being sure that each vowel is correctly placed before passing to the next. The proper use of the lips will aid greatly in focusing the vowels. Start with the scale that is in comfortable range.

a)
b)
Hung - ee - oo - oh-aw - ah
Hung - ee - oo-oh-aw - ah.
c)
d)
Hung - ee - oo - oh - aw - ah
Hung - ee - oo - oh-aw - ah
e)
f)
Hung - ee - oo - oh - aw - ah
Hung - ee - oo - oh-aw - ah
a)
b)
Hung - ee - oo - oh aw - ah
Hung - ee - oo-oh- aw - ah
c)
d)
Hung - ee - oo - oh-aw - ah
Hung - ee - oo - oh - aw - ah.

Exercise VIII

TO ENLARGE THE THROAT AND FOCUS THE VOWELS

Open the mouth well and be sure that the vowel sounds are delivered as in the previous exercises; this will insure largeness with proper resonance.

When practising this exercise, be careful, as with the others, that each vowel sound in its order is correctly given before passing to the next. Only in this way can rapid progress be made.

The words *bing*, *sing*, *ting*, *fling*, *swing* are excellent to use for further practice.

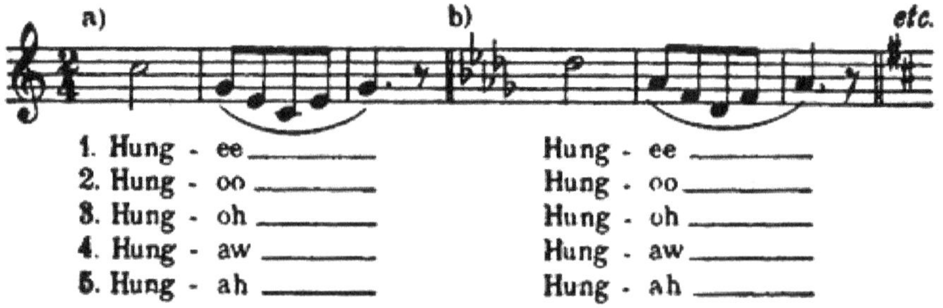

[Pg 67]

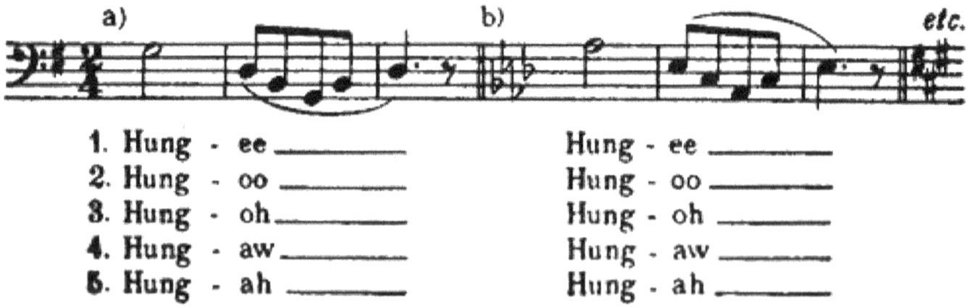

Exercise IX

QUICK CHANGING

NOTES WITHOUT CHANGING RESONANCE

The important point in this flexible exercise is to *keep the vowel-color, the focus or resonance, unchanged throughout the phrase*. Begin quietly, give the *ng* freedom and the upper resonance will adjust itself. This phrase is longer than in previous exercises; be sure then that you still have breath at the end—breath enough to sing further. Sing quietly. Pitch the exercise to suit the voice.

Exercise X

FOR AGILITY

Sing each vowel sound separately before passing to the next. Be sure to start each vowel sound in purity and maintain it without change. Pitch the exercise to suit the voice.

For variants on the above use as initial consonants *b*, *p*, *m*, *f*, *v*, *d*, *k*, *n*, *t*, and *l*.

Exercise XI

TO DEVELOP THE USE OF THE LIPS AND UNDER JAW

When practising this exercise protrude the lips and raise them toward the nose as far as possible; also make an effort to enlarge and widen the nostrils. This exercise may be practised more quickly than the preceding, but never at the expense of clearness of vowel distinction. Carry the exercise higher or lower, and in different keys, to suit individual voices. With a slight initial accent sing each two-measure section smoothly as one phrase. Avoid accenting each separate vowel sound. To do so would produce a series of jerks.

After practising the above as written modify it as follows:

1. Bee-boo-boh-baw-bah.
2. Pee-poo-poh-paw-pah.
3. Mee-moo-moh-maw-mah.
4. Fee-foo-foh-faw-fah.
5. Vee-voo-voh-vaw-vah.
6. Dee-doo-doh-daw-dah.
7. Kee-koo-koh-kaw-kah.
8. Nee-noo-noh-naw-nah.
9. Tee-too-toh-taw-tah.
10. Lee-loo-loh-law-lah.

Exercise XII

FOR FACILITY AND QUICK VOWEL CHANGE

Be careful not to blur the vowel sounds; each must be distinct and pure, and the change from one to the next must be made with a minimum of effort and without disturbing the focus of the tone.

The divisions (*a* and *b*) of each of the above four variants may be regarded as distinct exercises or not. For further practice use as initial consonants any or all of the following: *b*, *p*, *m*, *f*, *v*, *d*, *k*, *n*, *t*, and *l*.

Exercise XIII

ASCENDING AND DESCENDING SCALE

As in the previous exercises practise quietly with unvarying focus and aim to finish the phrase with breath unexhausted. Pitch the exercise to suit the voice.

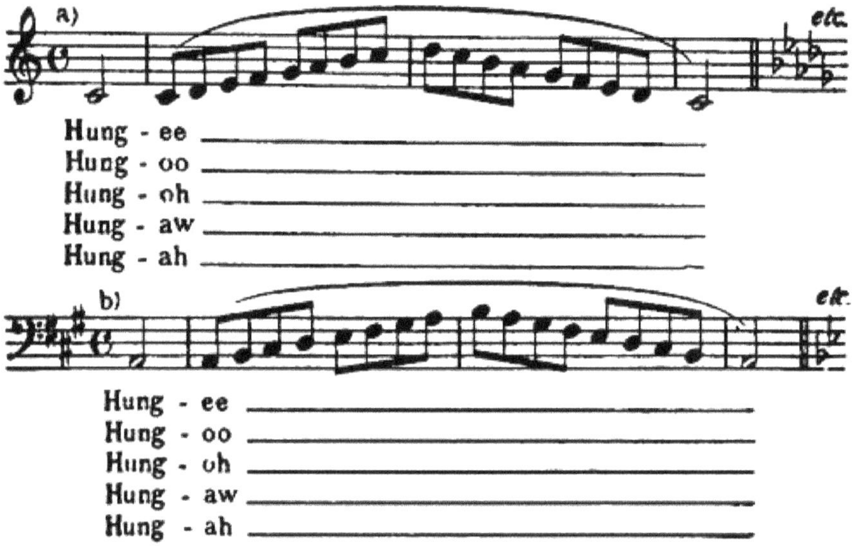

Exercise XIV

THE LONG SCALE

Sing this scale exercise in medium range, without blurring either the vowel sounds or the notes.

The exercises thus far given have employed the five vowel sounds found most helpful in gaining a free resonance. These should now be supplemented by the use of *all* the vowel sounds. It is obvious that unless the singer is at home with every vowel and on any pitch in his vocal range perfect pronunciation is impossible. In Chapter II a Scale of Vowel Sounds is given. For convenience it is repeated here:

nee,	**nit**,	***net***,	***nay***,	***nair***,	***nat***,	***nigh***,	***Nah***,	***not***,	***naw***,	***ner***,	***nut***,	***no***,	***nook***,	***noo***.
1	2	3	4	5	6	7	8	7′	6′	5′	4′	3′	2′	1′

Having so far mastered the previous exercises as to establish a free head and nasal resonance, take the Scale of Vowel Sounds and apply it to the now familiar exercises.

Next, as suggested in Exercise X, use as initial consonants in connection with the Vowel Scale the consonants *b, p, m, f, v, d, k, n, t* and *l*.

Keep before you the formula that articulation should *seem* to be done entirely with and through the upper lip; *i.e.*, the *thought* should be that the words are projected through the upper lip.

When by practise of the exercises given the voice has been focused and resonance established without any instrument,[Pg 73] scale exercises and simple vocalises may be taken up with or without the piano.

In practising scales start each a semitone higher until the *easy limit* of the voice is reached, and no farther. Gain will be more rapid by working to deliver the tones within the voice's normal compass. Then when occasional effort is made the organs will be found ready to deliver the highest pitch of which the voice is capable.

When sufficient progress has been made in mastering the execution of scales and easy vocalises, the pupil will be ready to begin the study of songs. If one foregoes the singing of songs during the few weeks occupied with primary lessons, results are obtained much more quickly.

While practising exercises or songs the less the pianoforte is used, except to compare the pitch, the better. Such practice increases the confidence of the performer. The instrument prevents the singer's listening to the tone he is producing and judging of its effectiveness.

Pupils with high or very low voices may continue their practice higher or lower as the voice is soprano, or bass, or contralto, but much practice on the extremes of the voice is unadvisable. If pure tones are produced in the medium range of the voice the highest or lowest tones will be found ready when called for. Therefore practise the extremes of the voice only enough to know the limits of the voice and to be assured the tones are there.

When the singer can perform the preceding simple exercises and know that the tones are all focused, or placed and delivered, precisely alike, he is ready to practise any scale, down or up, and to execute any musical exercise or song for which he is intellectually fitted.

CHAPTER IX
THROAT STIFFNESS

WHAT is the most frequent obstacle to good singing, the difficulty with which pupil and teacher most contend? Throat stiffness. What more than anything else mars the singing of those we hear in drawing-rooms, churches, and the concert room? Throat stiffness.

This is the vice that prevents true intonation, robs the voice of its expressiveness, limits its range, lessens its flexibility, diminishes its volume, and makes true resonance impossible.

This great interferer not only lessens the beauty of any voice, but directly affects the organ itself. The muscles of the larynx are small and delicate, and the adjustments they make in singing are exceedingly fine. When, however, the voice user stiffens his throat, these delicate muscles in their spontaneous effort to make the proper adjustments are compelled to contract with more than their normal strength. Every increase in throat stiffness demands a corresponding increase in muscle effort, an overexertion that persisted in must result in injury to the organ itself. Such misuse of the voice is bound to show injurious results. Every throat specialist knows this, and an untold multitude of those who, beginning with promise, have had to give up singing as a career, learn it too late.

Singers are so accustomed to the sound of their own voices as to be usually quite unconscious of their own throat stiffness, though they may recognize it in their neighbor.

Unfortunately throat stiffness by its very nature tends to aggravate itself, to constantly increase while the voice becomes less and less responsive to the singer's demands.

There are a number of contributing causes to throat stiffness, but the principal cause is *throat consciousness* and mis[Pg 75]placed effort, due largely to current misconceptions regarding the voice. A common notion is that we sing with the throat, whereas we sing *through* it. Akin to this error is the notion, as common as it is fallacious, that force of tone, carrying power, originates in the larynx, whereas the initial tone due to the vibration of the vocal cords is in itself comparatively feeble. As shown at length in Chapters VI and VII, volume of tone, its color and carrying power, is acoustically and vocally a matter of *resonance*.

Many there are who sing by dint of sheer force and ignorance, but their careers are necessarily short. The too common vulgar striving for power rather than for beauty or purity of tone induces unnatural effort and strain that both directly and sympathetically affect the throat with stiffness.

Unnatural effort in breathing, over-effort in breath control, as well as singing without adequate breath, all induce tension that is reflected at once in the sensitive throat.

Impatience of results, American hurry, beget unnatural effort and tension. "Unclasp the fingers of a rigid civilization from off your throat." The student of the violin or the piano soon learns that only by a long and patient preparation can he fit himself to entertain even his admiring friends. The embryo singer, on the contrary, expects with far less expenditure of time and effort to appear in public.

The human voice is a direct expression of the man himself; it registers spontaneously his mental and emotional states, even when he would wish them hidden. Mental conditions tinged with impatience, with fear, or with anything that begets tension of any sort are reflected instantly in the voice, robbing it of its better qualities and inducing stiffness in the throat.

Reduced to its lowest terms voice culture to-day is a struggle with throat stiffness.

The causes indicate the remedy. Foremost, then, is dropping all throat consciousness, all thought of the throat, all drawing of attention to it. The larynx must be left uncramped, unhindered to do its work in free unconsciousness,[Pg 76] which it will do if not disturbed by tension in its neighborhood, or by misdirected thought.

The stream of consciousness must in singing be directed to the breathing which is below the throat, and to resonance and pronunciation which are above it. These functions are more or less consciously controlled until at last mastery makes their action automatic.

I would once more emphasize the fact that the free use of all the resonance chambers, and the recognition of the great function of resonance, will do more than anything else to set the voice free and emancipate the singer from all interfering rigidity.

CHAPTER X

SOME GENERAL CONSIDERATIONS

THE NATURAL VOICE

PUPILS are constantly urged to sing and speak naturally, because the "natural" tone is correct. This is exceedingly indefinite. It is natural for a child to imitate the first sound it hears, whether it be correct or incorrect. In either case the child imitates it, and for that child it becomes the natural tone. The child reared in the wilderness, beyond the hearing of a human voice, will imitate the notes of the whip-poor-will, the chatter of the monkey, and the hoot of the owl, and for him they are natural tones.

To be natural is the hardest lesson to learn and it is only the result of imitation or prolonged discipline. Untrained naturalness is the perfection of awkwardness. The involuntary functions of organic life are the only ones naturally performed correctly. Nature's method of breathing, circulation, and digestion can be depended upon until disarranged by subsequent conditions, but unless proper vocalization is established by imitation and discipline this function is sure to be corrupted by false examples.

AGE TO BEGIN

After the child begins to talk, the sooner his vocal education begins the better. Even at that early age he can be made to understand the merits of head vibrations and by simple exercises produce them, and once taught will never forget them. Vocalizing, like every other art, is most easily learned by imitation, and the advantage of the early years, when that faculty is most active, should not be lost. In olden times the importance of this was fully realized. More than three centuries ago, old Roger Ascham wrote: "All languages, both[Pg 78] learned and mother tongues, are begotten and gotten solely by imitation. For as ye used to hear so ye learn to speak. If ye hear no other, ye speak not yourself; and of whom ye only hear, of them ye only learn." Nineteen centuries ago Quintillian wrote: "Before all let the nurses speak properly. The boy will hear them first and will try to shape his words by imitating them."

If the right way of using the voice is early taught it will be a guard against the contraction of bad habits which can only be corrected later with infinite trouble. It certainly would be unwise to put a young child under continued training; but even in the kindergarten the right method of voice production can and should be taught. Teachers of kindergarten and primary schools should be familiar with the principles of voice training and be able to start the pupils at once on the right road.

IN PUBLIC SCHOOLS

The sooner this branch of education is made a part of the curriculum of our common schools, the sooner shall we produce a race of good speakers and singers.

If, during the pupil's school life, proper attention is paid to these primary principles and to *correct articulation*, a large majority of students will graduate from our common schools prepared to advance in the art of elocution or of singing without being obliged first to unlearn a vast amount of error and to correct a long list of bad habits.

If each day in the public schools a few minutes only are devoted to the subject by a teacher who understands it and who will call the attention of the pupils to the proper applications of the principles in their daily recitations, it will be found amply sufficient to develop and establish a good speaking and singing voice.

ARTISTRY

If artistry is to be attained, every organ must be individually well trained. Yet, during performance, no one part[Pg 79] should be given undue prominence. The voice should be the product of all the organs equally well developed. Continued practice will enable the performer to correlate the whole—blend the strength of all in one.

It goes without saying that no one in singing or speaking should appear to be governed by a "method." During the early stages of education, pupils should be amenable to rules and methods, but they must not expect to be acceptable performers until able to forget their lessons and simply and unconsciously make use of all the advantages of their training. Even when the education is finished, and the *prima donna* has made her successful debut, continued daily repetition of primary exercises is necessary to maintain excellence and insure the progress that every performer desires. Our best singers to-day are as diligent students of the technique of the voice as are the tyros struggling with the first elements.

LIFE'S PERIODS

Human life is divided into three periods: *first*, that of effort to get an education; *second*, of effort to maintain it; and *third*, of effort to resist the natural decline which comes with advancing years. The singer and speaker must drill to develop the voice, must drill to keep it in condition, and must drill to resist the encroachments of senility. Eternal vigilance is the price of vocal success.

APPLICATION OF ESSENTIALS

The application of the principles here discussed will show that a musical voice is not the product of mysterious systems, but a matter of scientific certainty. The essentials are good breathing, good focusing, good resonance, and good articulation. These four elements are so interdependent that one cannot be perfected without the other. With these attained, the intellect, the sentiment, and the emotion of the performer will culminate in artistic excellence.[Pg 80]

REPOSE AS A PREPARATION FOR VOCAL EXERCISE

The nervousness or fear which manifests itself in constraint and rigidity of the muscles and sometimes in stage fright is a serious hindrance to progress. The effectual offset to this painful condition is repose.

The art of inducing a condition of repose can be readily acquired by any one who will carefully and faithfully do as follows: Place yourself in an easy lying or lounging position in a quiet place, with fresh air. Physical repose prepares for and invites mental repose. Now allow the mind to work care free at its own sweet will without any attempt to control it. Close the eyes and *breathe slowly, gently, and deeply, with steady rhythm.* In two or three minutes a sensation of quiet restful repose will be experienced, which may be continued for several minutes or may even lead to a natural sound sleep.

This result may not be attained at the first or the second trial, but a few repetitions of the exercise will insure success in almost every case. After the art is attained in this formal way, ability to induce the same repose when sitting upright, or while standing, will be quickly developed.

This repose is the fitting preparation for a lesson or a performance and may be induced during the progress of either, to allay any trepidation incident to the situation. A mastery of this simple art will make progress in the work of voice development much more rapid, and make attainable a degree of discipline that is impossible without it. It will prove for the beginner a sure prevention of stage fright and a great relief to the most chronic sufferer from this malady.

THE VIBRATO

The *vibrato* is a rhythmic pulsation of the voice. It often appears in untrained voices; in others it appears during the process of cultivation. Some have thought it the perfection of sympathetic quality; others esteem it a fault.

The vibrato is caused by an undulating variation of pitch or power, often both. The voice does not hold steadily and[Pg 81] strictly to the pitch, and according to the amount of the variation a corresponding vibrato, or tremolo, is produced.

The action of stringed instruments illustrates this statement. The finger of the violinist vibrates on the string by rocking rapidly back and forth and the vibrato is the result.

The same is true of the human instrument. By variation of the tension, the vocal apparatus sends forth several tones in alternation, of a slightly different pitch, which together produce the effect.

Three sources are ascribed for the vibrato; one is a rapid, spasmodic vibration of the diaphragm, causing variation of breath pressure; another is the alternate tension and relaxation of the larynx and vocal cords; a third is that commonest of faults—throat stiffness. Either cause is possible, and variation in the pitch or intensity of the tone is the result. Sufficient investigations have not been made to make the matter certain, but tremolo, trembling of the vocal organs, and muscular stiffness, or unnatural tension, seem to go together.

It is quite possible in the early stages of culture so to train the voice as to use the vibrato or not at will, but if not early controlled this, like other bad habits, gains the mastery. Excessive vibrato has spoiled many good voices. It is not a fundamental quality of the voice. A little vibrato may occasionally be desirable when properly and skilfully used; more than this is to be shunned as a dangerous vice.

CHAPTER XI
THE PSYCHOLOGY OF VOCAL CULTURE

MENTAL conception precedes execution. The picture must exist in the artist's mind before it can be drawn on the canvas. The architect must mentally see the majestic cathedral in all its details before he can draw the plans from which it can be built. In the field of physical activity no movement is made until the mind has gone before and prepared the way. A person's ability to do is in a great degree measured by his determination to do, but sitting in a rocking-chair and thinking will never make an athlete. Mental action is necessary, but only through trained muscular action can the mental action materialize in a finished performance.

So too the mind must anticipate the action of the vocal organs, but the organs themselves must be led to interpret the mental concept until such action becomes spontaneous. Action in turn quickens the mental process, and the mental picture becomes more vivid.

Note with emphasis that the mental concept *precedes* the action and governs it. Therefore, instead of producing tone by local effort, by conscious muscular action of any sort, correctly *think the tone*, correctly shape and color it *mentally*. **Every vocal tone is a mental concept made audible.** The beginner and the confirmed bungler alike fail in this prime essential—they do not make this mental picture of tone before singing it. Kindred to this is deficiency in hearing, in discriminating between good tone color and poor. The student must constantly compare his tone as it is sung with the picture in his mind. Training the voice is therefore largely a training of mind and ear, a developing of nicety in discrimination. Singing is mental rather than physical, psychologic rather than physiologic. Think therefore of the effect desired rather than of the process.[Pg 83]

In considering the details of voice production analytically we are apt to forget that man, notwithstanding his complexity, is a *unit* and acts as a unit. Back of all and underlying man's varied activity is the psychical. In the advanced stages of the art of speech and song this psychical element is of pre-eminent importance.

The speaker who essays to give expression to his own thoughts must have his ideas sharply defined and aflame in order to so utter them that they will arouse his hearers to enthusiasm. The speaker or singer who would successfully interpret the thoughts of others must first make those thoughts his very own. When this is attained, then the voice, action, and the whole spirit of the performer, responding to the theme, will beget a like responsiveness in his audience.

THE SINGER BEHIND THE VOICE

Books upon books have been written on voice training, and will continue to be written. The preceding pages have been devoted to the fundamental subject of tone production, but it is time to suggest that back of the voice and the song is the singer himself with his complex personality. Back of the personality is the soul itself, forever seeking utterance through its mask of personality. All genuine impulse to sing is from the soul in its need for expression. Through expression comes growth in soul consciousness and desire for greater and greater self-expression.

Singing is far more than "wind and muscle," for, as Ffrangcon-Davies puts it, "The whole spiritual system, spirit, mind, sense, *soul*, together with the whole muscular system from feet to head, will be in the wise man's singing, *and the whole man will be in the tone*."

Of all the expressions of the human spirit in art form, the sublimated speech we call song is the most direct. Every other art requires some material medium for its transmission, and in music, subtlest of all the arts, instruments are needed, except in singing only.

FREEDOM

In song the singer himself is the instrument of free and direct expression. Freedom of expression, complete utterance, is prevented only by the singer himself. No one hinders him, no one stands in the way but himself. The business of the teacher is to *set free* that which is latent. His high calling is by wise guidance to help the singer to get out of his own way, to cease standing in front of himself. Technical training is not all in all. Simple recognition of the existence of our powers is needed even more. Freedom comes through the recognition and appropriation of inherent power; recognition comes first, the appropriation then follows simply. The novice does not know his natural power, his birthright, and must be helped to find it, chiefly, however, by helping himself, by cognizing and re-cognizing it.

No student of the most human of all arts—singing—need give up if he has burning within him the *song impulse*, the *hunger to sing*. This inner impulse is by its strength an evidence of the power to sing; the very hunger is a promise and a prophecy.

DETERRENTS

The deterrents to beautiful singing are physical in appearance, but these are outer signs of mental or emotional disturbance. Normal poise, which is strength, smilingly expresses itself in curves, in tones of beauty.

Mental discord results in angularity, rigidity, harshness.

Impatience produces feverishness that makes vocal poise impossible; and impatience induces the modern vice of forcing the tone. Growth is a factor for which hurried forcing methods make no allowance.

Excess of emotion with its loss of balance affects the breathing and play of the voice.

Exertion, trying effort, instead of easy, happy activity induces hampering rigidities.

Intensity, over-concentration, or rather false concentra[Pg 85]tion, emotional tension, involves strain, and strain is always wrong.

Over-conscientiousness, with its fussiness about petty detail, and insistence on non-essentials, is a deterrent from which the robust are free. *Over-attention to the mechanics* of voice production is a kindred deterrent. Both deterrents prevent that prime characteristic of expression—spontaneity.

Anxiety is a great contractor of muscle, a great stiffener. Anxiety always forgets the *power* within, and falsely says to the song-hunger, "You shall never be satisfied."

Self-repression is a great deterrent that afflicts the more sensitive, particularly those of puritanic inheritance. It is a devitalizer and a direct negative to expression, which is vital, is *life*.

All of these deterrents are negative and may be overcome by fuller recognition of the inner power that by its very nature must perpetually seek positive expression.

CONCLUSION

In conclusion, the student can perpetually find encouragement in a number of happy facts.

Man is endowed by nature, except in rare instances, with a perfect vocal apparatus. When abnormal conditions are found they are usually in the adult voice, and are due solely to misuse. In other words defects are not inherent but acquired and *can be removed.*

By nature the human voice is beautiful, for the tendency of nature is always in the direction of beauty. Whatever is unlovely in singing, as in all else, is *un*natural. True method is therefore never artificial in its action, but simple, because the natural is always simple.

Finally, no, not finally, but firstly and secondly and thirdly and perpetually, every student of singing and every teacher of it must constantly bear in mind the happy law:

THE RIGHT WAY IS ALWAYS AN EASY WAY

www.ingramcontent.com/pod-product-compliance
Lightning Source LLC
Chambersburg PA
CBHW071101090426
42737CB00013B/2425
* 9 7 8 1 9 3 6 8 2 8 1 8 0 *